102 Models of Procurement & Supply Chain Management

Second Edition reflecting CIPS New Syllabus

Paul Jackson & Barry Crocker

Cambridge Academic

Imprints include:
Liverpool Academic Press
Liverpool Business Publishing
Tudor Educational

© 2021 Paul Jackson & Barry Crocker

The rights of Jackson & Crocker to be identified as the authors of this work have been asserted by them in accordance with the Copyright, Designs and Patents Act 1988.

All rights reserved. No part of this publication may be reproduced, stored in a retrieval system, or transmitted in any form or by any means, electronic, mechanical, photocopied, recorded, or otherwise without prior permission of Cambridge Academic at:
The Studio, High Green, Gt. Shelford, Cambridge. CB22 5EG

ISBN 10: 1903-500-56-7
ISBN 13: 978-1903-500-56-9

The contents of this publication are provided in good faith and neither The Author nor The Publisher can be held responsible for any errors or omissions contained herein. Any person relying upon the information must independently satisfy himself or herself as to the safety or any other implications of acting upon such information and no liability shall be accepted either by The Author or The Publisher in the event of reliance upon such information nor for any damage or injury arising from any interpretation of its contents. This publication may not be used in any process of risk assessment.

Printed and bound in the United Kingdom by 4edge Ltd, 22 Eldon Way Industrial Estate, Hockley, Essex, SS5 4AD.

Contents

Preface i
Who is this book for? ii
Introduction iv
What exactly does this book contain? vi
Student Guidance 1
Procurement & Supply Chain Models 27
Business Analysis Models 31
Category Management Models 39
Contract & Change Management Models 45
Cost & Value Models 51
Ethical & Environmental Models 57
Human Resource Management Models 67
Management & Leadership Models 79
Market & Price Analysis Models 101
Procurement Models 109
Quality Models 121
Relationship & Stakeholder Models 129
Risk Models 141
Strategic Supply Chain Management Models 147
Conclusion 153
Resources 155
Bibliography 159

Preface

During our teaching and consultancy work over the years, we have seen the use and application of many Procurement, Supply Chain and Management models. These models help the user understand, evaluate or position features and characteristics to enable a more considered assessment and diagnosis throughout the Procurement process.

More importantly they add structure to reports, marks to exam answers and substance to assignments.

Aside from updating and realigning the content to the revised academic syllabi, our endeavour with this second edition is to expand on our 2015 publication to give extra depth and attention to the use of the main models within the structure of distinction and A* grade assignments and exam responses.

Further, at the request of a significant number of students during our academic delivery, we have included ideas and additional guidance useful for attainment of extra marks and higher grades.

Finally, we would like to thank Ray Carter for his motivation during the writing of the first edition and for the continued use of his models in this second edition.

Who Is This Book For?

A fundamental question for any aspiring author is "who will read my book?"

Clearly, without a defined understanding of "the who", a text can become distracted and lose sight of its intended objectives.

We have however learned and taken notice of the feedback following the first edition and have endeavoured to reflect those comments. Aside from updating the list of models, we have also added some preliminary text relating to exam strategy and development for student readers, and highlighted aspects aside from the core models where students can secure additional marks and enhance their results.

These aspects include details of example organisations, legislation, electronic systems, data capture, reporting and the presentation of results.

In short, therefore, this book is intended for all of the following readership groups:

- **Students** studying for Procurement, Supply Chain, Logistics, general business management, sales, and other related courses or examinations.
- **Practitioners** looking to improve operational or commercial performance through the use of internationally recognised models proven to increase efficiency, raise awareness of issues, reduce waste, exploit opportunities, manage risk, and so on.
- **Management** looking to evaluate performance, exploit external opportunities and generate strategy to deliver the corporate vision.
- **Sales** personnel and anybody else with a corporate interest in evaluating the actions of others with a view to determining their strategic ambitions.

Introduction

Following the success of the first edition of this book, coupled with the updating of a number of academic syllabi including most notably the CIPS syllabus, it has been decided the models should be reviewed to meet the latest student and practitioner needs.

That is not to say that any of the models included in the previous edition have in any way become defunct, more that new models have entered the field of academic thinking which may offer the reader a different, extended or updated perspective.

The concept of Procurement and Supply Chain Management is a well-recognised and defined profession with established processes and infrastructure. Its cross-functional contribution and its need to engage stakeholders from both within and outside the organisation makes it core to the development of strategy and delivery of successful outcomes throughout.

As an industry, the development of models, tools and processes to help illustrate opportunities, drive analysis, dissect problems and generate strategic philosophy is fundamental to its success, with the overall objective of:

- Reducing cost whilst improving quality;
- Improving flexibility and speed of throughput;
- Development of new products and market share;
- Enhancement of brand development and customer relationships;
- Delivery of exceptional customer service;
- Focussing on effectiveness and efficiency;
- Generating a culture of staff empowerment;
- And nurturing a focus on continuous improvement.

Note: The aforementioned list is worthy of note for any aspiring student as this in itself offers a clear list of possible opportunities to contribute value within an effective commercial function.

Further, since the first edition of this book, there has been a steady and sustained increase in the focus on the importance of maintaining an ethical operation cognisant of the need to remain compliant with international regulations and UN legislation designed to address global commercial issues such as slavery, child labour, corruption and other unethical behaviours. In line with this focus, the main academic institutions have heightened their syllabi content with exam and assignment content rewarded accordingly; this change has thus been mirrored in this second edition with the introduction of a separate section addressing this critical facet of the current operating climate.

In recent years, the extent and breadth of the contribution of the Procurement and Supply Chain Management function to the operation of the organisation has become more visible and better publicised. This has inevitably led to increased investment in training and development and has led to a rise in organisations supporting and underpinning the industry, organisations such as CIPS, IACCM, ISM, IIAPS, IFPSM, PASIA and a host of other international and regional institutions.

All the main Procurement and Supply Chain institutions incorporate structure and mechanism to enable the training and development of their members with qualifications, examinations and CPD (Continuous Profession Development) activities at their core. These development constructs utilise many of the popular business models, yet few publications are readily available to succinctly collate these models in a user-friendly yet affordable manner.

And remember, in exams "Models Mean Marks".

And therein lies the motivation and challenge embraced by the authors; our intention with this publication is therefore summarised as follows:

1. To collate the most common, popular and effective Procurement and Supply Chain models into one publication;
2. To remain succinct in the definition, explanation and critique of each model;
3. To remain an affordable, concise and user-friendly publication both to students and practitioners.

What Exactly Does This Book Contain?

In short, this publication contains a revised combination of 102 diverse and cross-functional models which the authors and some of their esteemed colleagues deem to be of greatest value, and which they have found to be of most use when working within global organisations, delivering consultancy activities or teaching Procurement and Supply Chain subjects to international students studying CIPS and other qualifications.

Each model or tool is contained within a single page, headed with a short definition, followed by further detail and explanation, analysis of any evolutions and iterations, with an "advantages and disadvantages" critique to conclude. A large number of the models are also then supported with an Instagram page entitled #ModelsofBusiness with all pictures redrawn by the authors; these drawings are available licence free to any student wishing to cut and paste them into a project or assignment.

Further, as a supplementary feature, the concepts are explored in a practical manner through the VidBlinqz learning support package available at www.vidblinqz.com. Persons purchasing this book can secure a 10% discount off the subscription fee by referencing the discount code MOPVBZ.

Student Exam Guidance

Understand the Syllabus

Whilst each Procurement and Supply Chain institution has its own anomalies within its own syllabus, the content of this book, by its very nature, applies equally across all. There is therefore no singularity of focus on any one syllabus or institution, nor is it intended that the content is necessarily restricted to these aforementioned groups. There are however some generic thoughts as to how models could be used to explore and develop exam answers, with many marking schemes having an allocation of marks to reward such usage, especially where the purpose of the assessment is to determine the diagnostic skills of the student against a specific case study or market scenario.

In conclusion therefore, this work reflects a clear need identified over many years of consultancy and teaching. We intend that this text is an affordable production full of common and popular models to help the user and student improve their lot.

Crafting An Effective Answer

When developing an exam response or an assignment submission, it is essential to generate a structure to the answer that gives the marker the confidence to reward the student.

When preparing an exam answer the use of examples and evidence to support a comment or point is essential to securing the additional marks necessary to move from a pass to a merit and onto a distinction.

Remember in a number of marking schemes the **PREM** concept is worth remembering: **Point – Reason – Example - Models**

In an exam you need to succinctly make your **POINT**. The POINT approach looks at the most effective way in which a piece of written information can be communicated to secure higher levels of marks. It considers the best way to make a message heard in either the text or indeed in oral presentations whilst helping the audience remember what was said. The approach considers five core elements remembered by the POINT acronym:

- **P - PREPARATION** Good preparation and a deliver strategy such as the Point-Reason-Example-Point method used by politicians helps generate a clear structure;
- **O - ONE PAGE** Make any document one page, any more and the message will be lost in the volume – a one-page document will always be read before a book, and the secret to being remembered is to be first, second or last, one page helps ensure this;
- **I - INTERESTING** Seems obvious, but make the text interesting otherwise it will go in one ear and out of the other;
- **N - NEWSWORTHY** Try and tie the message into a recent event, a piece of news or the current corporate endeavour to add impact;
- **T - THREE** Finally do not make it too complicated, use The Power of Three - A brain becomes muddled when there are more than three points, three colours (including the background even if it's white), sizes or types of text, and any other visual facets, so help your reader's brain function.

Refer To The Procurement Process

In most commercial and Public Sector environments there is an agreed procurement process, albeit in the Public Sector, Defence and Utilities domains the approach is far more regulated and often mandated. These processes – for example OJEU, Utilities Contracting Regulations, the Defence Regulations - steer the day-to-day activity and strategy, as well as creating robust structure.

Whilst there are a number of different variants adopted between organisations, institutes, jurisdictions, nations and trading-blocks such as the EU, the structure of the procurement process (See figure i) and the fundamental chain of events is fairly standard with the same overall objective of:

1) Securing some form of goods, utilities or services to fulfil a need;
2) In a compliant, fair and equitable manner;

3) Whilst recognising the basic Five Rights;
4) And ensuring best use of corporate or public resources.

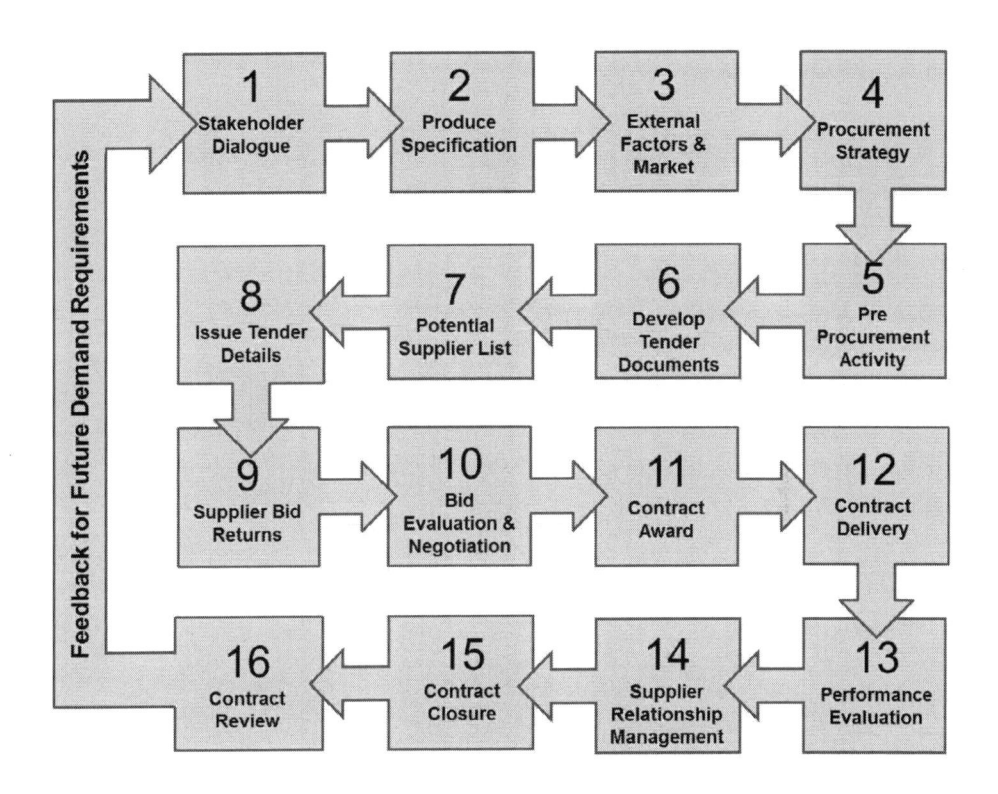

Figure i – A Typical Procurement Process

Procurement process flow diagram with 16 steps:
1. Stakeholder Dialogue
2. Produce Specification
3. External Factors & Market
4. Procurement Strategy
5. Pre Procurement Activity
6. Develop Tender Documents
7. Potential Supplier List
8. Issue Tender Details
9. Supplier Bid Returns
10. Bid Evaluation & Negotiation
11. Contract Award
12. Contract Delivery
13. Performance Evaluation
14. Supplier Relationship Management
15. Contract Closure
16. Contract Review

With "Feedback for Future Demand Requirements" looping back to the start.

The Procurement process should be clearly defined, consistent and users trained in its operation, and will need input and assessments throughout its operation, incorporating many of the models contained within this book.

Choose Your Models Wisely & Use The Latest Variant

Over time, some models have become widely understood and used – for example the SWOT analysis to assess the internal features of an organisation, project, team, function or other group has morphed and is often now used in the TOWS format – whilst others have evolved as the needs of the user have changed – for example PEST, became SLEPT, became PESTLE, became STEEPLE, and is now STEEPLED.

For the user, understanding the portfolio of models – as well as any iterations that have evolved – is critical if the corporate resource is to be used to full effect. Many models have blurred edges or vagaries in their objectives, whilst others are arguably just mutations or reinventions of other similar models.

Within this sea of models there are, however, some models which are fundamental to the success of an organisation or protagonists therein. Many of these - for example Porter's Five Forces in the evaluation of a market – have been instrumental in developing how aspects are viewed and appraised. Such models, whilst commonly recognised and appreciated, formed the initial foundations of this work, created in the first instance to assist Procurement students in Nigeria understand the models that could be used within international Procurement, Supply Chain, and management examinations to help develop answers and gain extra marks.

Some considerable dialogue and deliberation were also undertaken as to the depth and extent that each model should reflect. Whilst there are other similar publications available over a greater depth of a few main models, our intention here is to provide a broad range of models with each review providing a succinct assessment of that model in a form that is both easy to absorb and retain on the part of the reader, whilst contained in length to ensure affordability recognising that for many this book should form an examination guide or aide memoire.

Understand The Contract Terms And Pricing

A key part of the Procurement function is the development and management of the Contract.

In our day-to-day commercial activities and within an exam setting, be ever mindful of the key aspects required to form a contract: Offer, Acceptance (Unconditional), Consideration, Intention, Capacity and Legality. If possible, ensure you have examples to support your answer, for e.g. case law examples, underpinning legislation, demonstration of intent and clarity over the transfer of value that forms the consideration.

Understanding some of the different types of contract and their structures is also useful. Typically, when we write a contract, we begin by establishing the Critical Success Factors however these need to be succinct and definitive. It has been suggested by some legal practitioners that there should be no more than five CRITICAL success factors in a Contract, and that these should then align with the Conditions of Contract therein. In legal terms, a breach of a "Condition can lead to the Cancellation of a Contract". A lesser term in a Contract is referred to as a Warranty and a "Warranty Won't cancel a contract" – see figure ii.

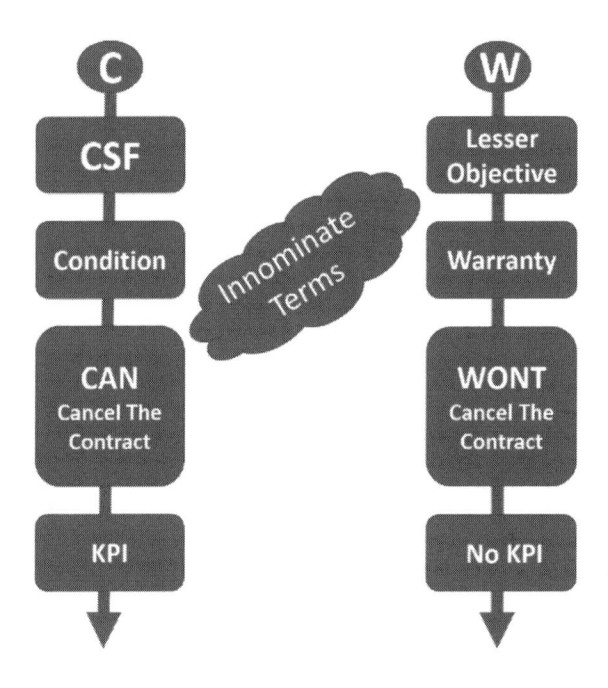

Figure ii – Warranties & Conditions and Contract Termination

Further, when we manage the Contract, we should focus on these critical aspects within the contractual objectives by assigning appropriate KPIs to enable us to deal most effectively with a contractor failing to fulfil the most essential aspects of their scope.

What is also useful to consider when addressing contractual issues is the choice of contract type and the pricing mechanisms utilised. In terms of the Contract, there are several generic types of contract including the following:

Bespoke Contracts – Those written especially for the situation, so reflect the specific requirements pertaining to the individual situation and the two contracting Parties. They are normally written on a case by case basis making them expensive to produce and often lacking in commonality of structure which can lead to confusion and challenges when they are managed over the Contract period;

Model Form Contracts – Generic contracts such as the NEC4 Contract with adjustable terms, often produced by reputable and independent third-parties like the Association of Consulting Engineers. These give a consistent structure and allow the two Parties to negotiate individual terms, often from a menu of pre-written clauses, though a failure to agree on any of the options provided within the template often results in the rewriting of some contentious clauses;

Standard Terms and Conditions – A non-negotiated standard contract produced by one of the Parties, although acceptance of these standard T&Cs is usually either through ignorance, complacency, laziness or if the other Party has excessive power in the relationship;

Framework Agreements – Strictly speaking, these can only be Agreements as there is no Consideration, a core requirement of a legally binding contract. The Framework Agreement becomes a Contract when a demand is placed against the Framework, that demand generating an individual Contract within the Framework.

Further, within the Procurement and Contractual understanding, it is important that the method of pricing undertaken by the Supplier is understood to determine the level of price surety, the allocation of risk, and the strategic intentions of the Supplier in the relationship.

There are many such pricing policies such as Cost-Plus Pricing, Penetration Pricing, Loss-Leaders, Market Pricing, or Skimming. A list and explanation are contained in figure iii:

Cost-Plus Pricing	• Price is the cost price of the goods or services with a profit margin added on.
Market Pricing	• Price is set to reflect the price levels in the market or that a customer will pay.
Market Penetration	• Price is set to below the prevailing market rate to gain market share.
Skimming	• High price set to gain high profit per unit during launch phase to recoup development costs.
Psychological Pricing	• Price is set just below psychological barriers typically of the form $19.99.
Value Based Pricing	• Price is calculated around the perceived value that the product gives the consumer.
Loss Leader	• Supplier sells below cost to generate market share to capture a competitive advantage.
Predatory Pricing	• Similar to Loss-Leader, but price is set very low (though not lossmaking) to poach business.

Figure iii – Pricing Strategies

Finally, the success and effectiveness of the contractual relationship evolves from the balance between the risk and values generated within the contract, however without a mutually acceptable balance between the Buyer and Supplier, the contractual relationship will struggle and prove unsustainable.

The Basis Of Ethical Procurement

A key aspect of modern Procurement and Supply Chain Management is the necessity to acknowledge and manage the ethical issues that may occur across the Supply Chain and indeed within the Buying Organisation itself.

Underpinned with significant levels and layers of legislative protection, the potential risks associated with ethical factors are substantial in terms of public relations and costs associated with fines and reparations. This may also involve numerous issues that could compromise an organisation's ability to deliver goods or services on time to customers and business partners; such challenges justify this as a critical 21st Century problem.

To begin with, in order to show credibility, it is important for an organisation to take an ethical stance and defining what ethical behaviour means should be a top priority; this definition is a useful construct to underpin an exam or assignment response.

By way of an example, the UN Procurement Directives suggest that there are two definitions of ethics as follows:

- The moral principles governing or influencing conduct.
- The branch of knowledge concerned with moral principles

The concept of moral principles – and indeed the concept of moral itself – is a difficult area to address in a global capacity. So much of our background, upbringing and community is involved in the generation of our Moral Compass, the part of our person which delineates between right and wrong, and as such this will differ around the world. Whilst ideally, a common approach to ethical best practice would be a useful baseline, the global perspective needs to be embraced, with global legislation and guidelines introduced to try and drive consistency and understanding.

From an organisational perspective, stating the moral and ethical stance is essential to inform both internal and external stakeholders of what is expected. Aspects such as transparency, integrity, treating people equitably and fairly form the basis of ethical best practice, however various pieces of legislation help generate substance as to what is expected.

The CIPS Code of Conduct is an example of what to expect in an ethical charter:

- Enhance and protect the standing of the profession
- Maintain the highest standard of integrity in all business relationships
- Promote the eradication of unethical business practices
- Enhance the proficiency and stature of the profession
- Ensure full compliance with laws and regulations

The CIPS Code of Conduct forms the corporate basis against which it generates policy and manages its operational activity, however the wider laws of the land need to be considered and complied with. International, regional, and local legislation includes the following which are useful, amongst others, to reference as examples in an exam environment:

- United Nations Universal Declaration of Human Rights
- Ethical Trading Initiative
- The UN Slavery Convention
- The UK Equalities Act 2010
- Transparency in Negotiation Act (TINA)

In summary therefore, the ethical code applies to the Organisation, the Suppliers and Customers in the wider Supply Chain. Issues such as human rights, slavery, child labour, commercial corruption and equitable treatment need to addressed. The ethical charter, effective auditing and analysis should be undertaken to ensure that these aspects are both compliant and developmental, improving people's lives and their community.

Accordingly, a diligent Procurement and Commercial operator will:

1. Ensure effective ethical leadership is appointed and visible throughout the commercial relationship;
2. Be ever mindful and tolerant of the culture and behaviours in which they are contracting whilst delivering commercial outcomes without the involvement of corrupt practices;
3. Ensure effective training and visibility of the ethical objectives is available for all, along with a clear understanding of the penalties for non-compliance;
4. Collect suitable data and detail on an ongoing basis to facilitate maintaining meaningful measurement and evaluation;
5. Use enforcement in a predetermined and consistent manner to ensure non-ethical practices are eliminated and negative outcomes are punished appropriately and proportionally.

In terms of an ethical exam or assignment answer, ensure that the concepts detailed hitherto are at the forefront of your mind, and be aware of some of the common terms related to corruption – see figure iv:

Figure iv – Areas of Ethical Malpractice

A number of these terms – for example Theft, Fraud, and Bribery - are commonly used in commercial circles, however Nepotism (favouring a friend or relative), Collusion (covertly working together without transparency), and Extortion (forcing a third party to do something against their will through a use of force, sometimes called Coercion) are less frequently understood.

Finally, be ever mindful that ethical practices and strategy need to reflect changes in legislation and other external factors. To drive the ethical agenda there needs to be a clear strategic plan and Board level intention with a cyclical approach involving clear definitions, training, audit arrangements, notifications, remedial actions and assigned responsibilities as shown in the Fraud and Corruption plan detailed in figure v.

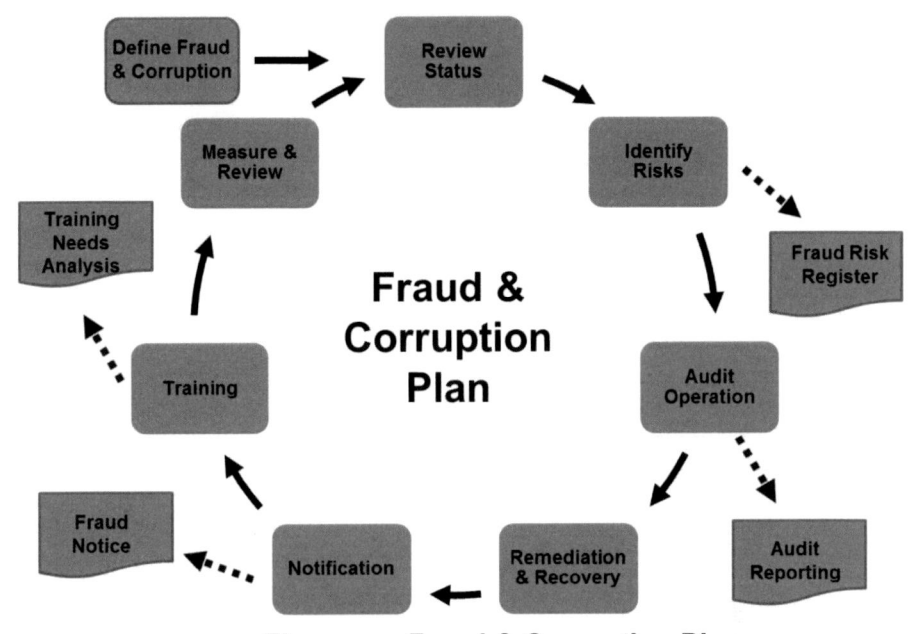

Figure v – Fraud & Corruption Plan

Such a focus ensures that the issue remains at the forefront of employees' minds, whilst tying the management of non-ethical behaviour into the risk process helps keep it within the regular process review mechanisms necessary for such an important part of an organisation's commercial delivery.

Know Your IT Systems

Good marks are often available for applying models and theory within the organisation's operating infrastructure. In exams, understanding the impact of IT systems (for example an ERP System as shown in figure vi), data collection, responsible data management and the legislative directives that might apply – for example ISO27000 or GDPR regulations – has proven fruitful in many instances as this gives the examiner a sense of a wider pool of application and knowledge. Referencing the use of data capturing solutions – for example, bar codes, RFID tags, or SIM Card Monitoring systems – can equally add additional depth to an answer. This shows a practical awareness of how data is used to manage a situation. Remember the CIPS adage – "if you can't measure it you can't manage it" – however, if you can't even collect data, the measurement will be unreliable and ineffective, and will thus give false direction within the management process.

Understanding how the IT system is embedded within the organisation's operational structure, and wider the use of paperwork systems to steer the audit function and generate traceability – see figure vi – gives useful substance when operational requirements are sought.

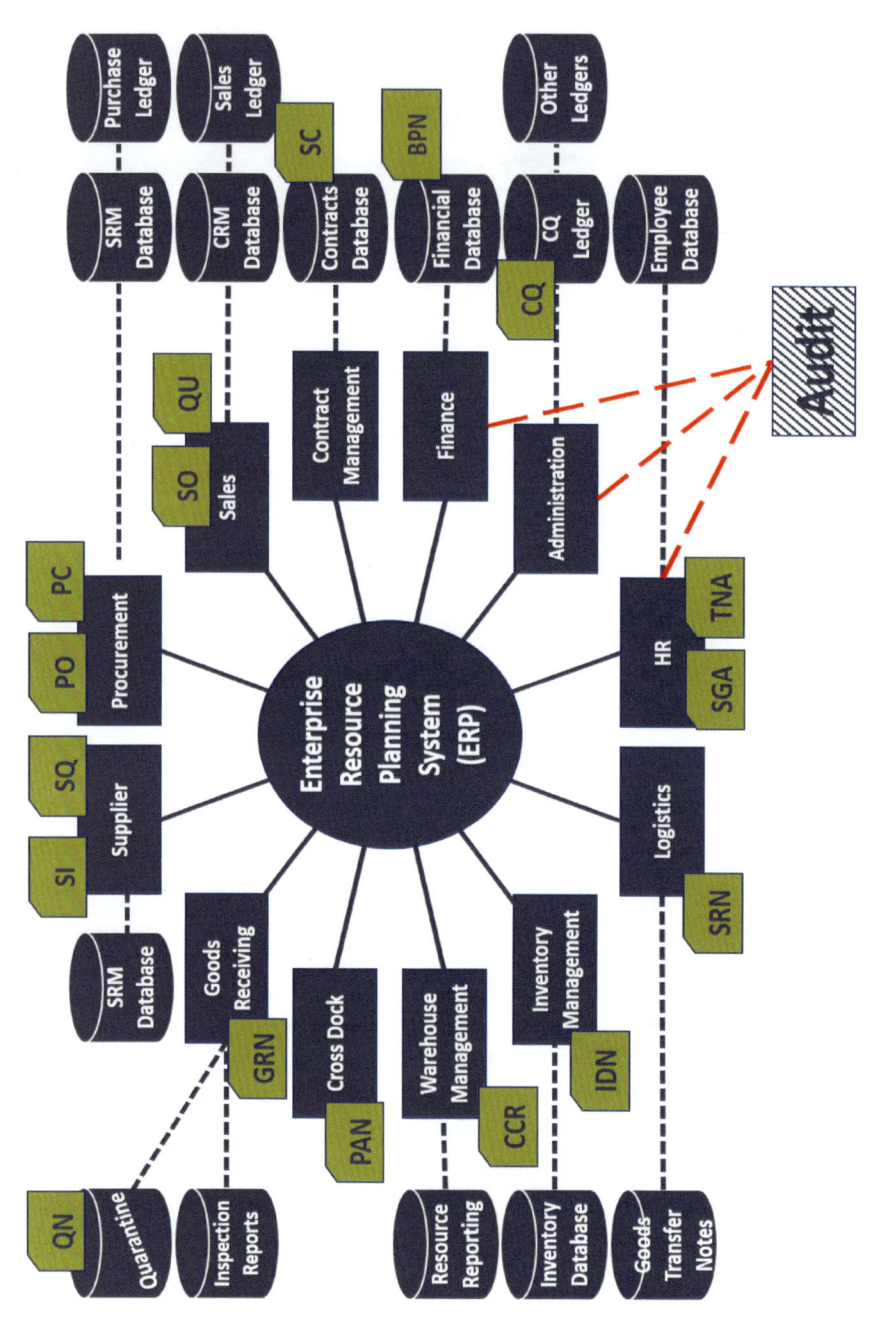

Figure vi – Example ERP Solution

Key to Documents

QU	Sales Quotation
GRN	Goods Receiving Note
SO	Sales Order
QN	Quarantine Notice
SC	Sales Contract
PAN	Put-Away Note
PO	Purchase Order
CCR	Cycle Count Request
PC	Purchase Contract
IDN	Inventory Discrepancy Notice
SI	Supplier Invoice
SRN	Shipping Request Notification
SQ	Supplier Quotation
BPN	Banking Payment Notices
SGA	Skills Gap Analysis
CQ	Commercial Query
TNA	Training Needs Analysis

When considering IT systems, a focus on the Value-Added by the system should be maintained both to ensure that effective and informed decisions are made within the organisations as well as enabling the ring-fencing and preservation of this value within the operating activities.

The Values generated by an IT system are often closely aligned with those generated by an effective procurement process, for example lower costs, reduced waste, better risk management, faster transaction times, shorter lead-times or better levels of communication. Some systems however focus on clear elements of the Supply Chain to effect and manage change, and enhance the end-to-end process and relationships therein.

A clear example of this is the P2P – Purchase-to-Pay – cycle which drives shorter and more efficient payment functions. This is often done with little more than the efficient transfer of notifications through the Supply Chain. The Three-Way Purchase Invoice Matching System (PIMS) is an example of this as shown in Figure vii.

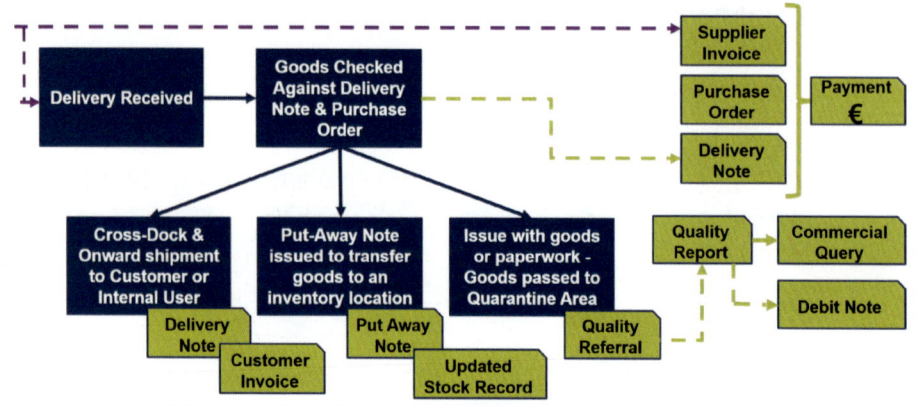

Figure vii – Example PIMS Paperwork Flow

In summary, the PIMS system simply collates and verifies the alignment between three documents:

- The Purchase Order;
- The Supplier's Invoice;
- The Goods Receiving Note.

In essence, this automates the check that confirms that the Procurement Five Rights – The Right Quantity of the Right Quality of goods was delivered at the Right Time to the Right Place and charged at the Right Price as per the agreed pricing arrangements – have been secured. In the event that the conditions of contract have been met, providing the value of the invoice is below a predetermined corporate threshold, payment is transmitted to the Supplier without further analysis.

Recognising that paying on time is a major component of supplier satisfaction and the "Attractiveness" dimension referred to in the Steele & Court Supplier Preferencing model, this prompt settlement of debt can be seen to have significant relationship and commercial benefits; this may also facilitate the securing of additional 30-day settlement discounts often offered by agents, wholesalers and other middlemen. Whilst traditional Finance Department operatives may seek to withhold payments until the last possible moment to aid cashflow, when deposit and loan interest rates are low, the values generated by low administrative payment systems and enhanced supplier relationships need to be closely considered.

International Trade & Logistics

In modern Procurement and Supply Chain Management, especially with high levels of Outsourcing and complex Supply Chains, the need to comprehend the import and export mechanisms designed to facilitate the flow of goods, trust and payment across international borders – whether transit occurs by land, sea or air – is imperative.

Of these, the first aspect that needs to be addressed is the trust between Buyer and Seller. Especially applicable with embryonic relationships, both parties will be looking to preserve their commercial position; buyers will be reluctant to pay up front, yet sellers/manufacturers will be reluctant to manufacture goods without some form of upfront commitment.

The lack of trust is not a new challenge and has historically been managed using independent and trusted third-parties – for example international Merchant Banks – to receive and hold money from the Buyer on behalf of the Seller in what is referred to as an Escrow Account, see figure viii.

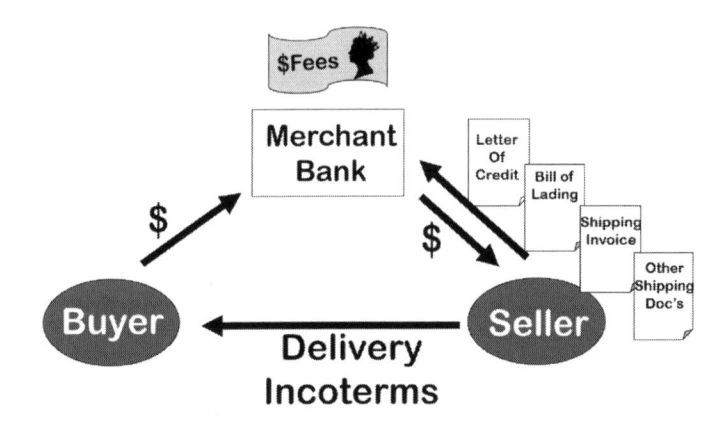

Figure viii – Flow of Funds using an Escrow Account

Very simply, once the funds have been received by the Merchant Bank and deposited in the Escrow Account, a Letter of Credit is raised informing the Seller what they need to do to release and trigger the transfer of the funds into their bank account. In figure viii, these requirements are listed as including the Shipping Invoice and Shipping Documents; Shipping Documents may include a Bill of Lading, Shipping Manifest, Air Waybill, Consignment Notes or Certificate of Origin.

It is also necessary in such transactions to determine the responsibilities of ownership, costs and liabilities during the transit of goods which can sometimes be quite challenging, time-consuming and costly. Incoterms are the primary mechanism or tool used in international trade (and indeed sometimes with intra-national logistics) for knowing who is responsible for what and when. They cover:

1. The point at which transfer of risk and responsibility occurs;
2. The responsibility for costs of insurance, administration and logistics;
3. Who will pay tax, levies and duties, and;
4. Liability for any issues caused, including accidents and environmental issues such as pollution.

Incoterms are invariably used in legal contracts, shipping directives, and negotiations but they are also a very good source of marks within an exam question covering such matters.

A significant number of different Incoterms are available at any given time and were last updated in 2020. These updates and amendments reflect changes in circumstances and the prevailing global geopolitics and trade situations. Some of these are shown in the figure ix, highlighting some example Incoterms at various points between the despatch gate of the Supplier (Ex-Works - EXW) and the point of delivery at the Buyer's premises with all taxes and levies paid (Delivery Duty Paid – DDP).

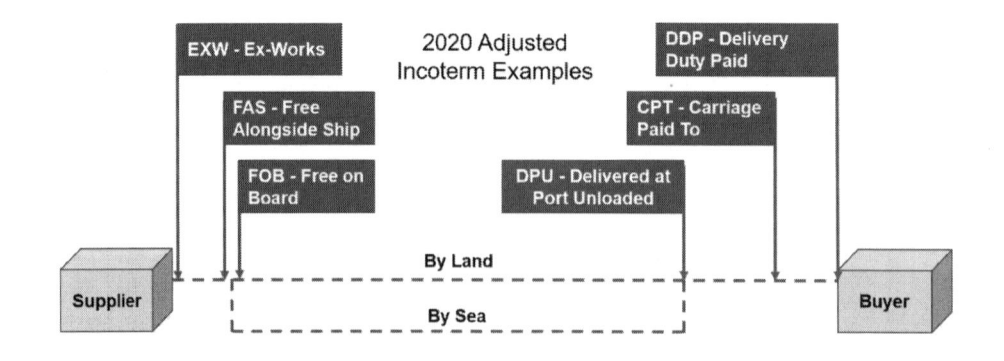

Figure ix - Incoterms

Finally, an important element of this transactional relationship that needs to be considered is the issue of fees. Clearly a Merchant Bank is a commercial operation and as such will charge for the Escrow services provided. These are commonly based on hours of work required to set up the arrangement rather than a percentage. As a result, charges vary but are often quite significant, especially when the value of the consignment is small, as is invariably the case with new relationships.

In contrast, transactions managed using Cryptocurrency and Blockchain services are now proving to be quicker, far more affordable, easier to manage and include a full end-to-end indelible traceability of process; as a result, a number of industries - for example the cotton industry – have adapted these virtual options within their day to day operation.

Using Data And Targeting

Utilisation of modern IT systems and data collection is an essential part of any 21st Century Procurement and Supply Chain Management activity. As mentioned hitherto, in many organisations, the IT systems both underpin and steer corporate structure and processes, with a significant percentage of organisations tending to produce processes that fit a generic off-the-shelf system as opposed to developing bespoke systems.

In the 1980s, when IT systems were in their infancy, the suggestion was that computer systems would quickly lead to a paperless office, devoid of clip binders with vast quantities of documents held solely on magnetic data. Whilst migration to such a utopia has been far slower than first envisaged, the advent of the Internet – along with software platforms such as Sharepoint and The Cloud – has steered a steady path thereto. Organisations using an ERP Solution however can often find that both the quantum of data collected and the reports generated appear useful, but still this can be the root cause of an information overload.

In data management be mindful of measuring only those aspects that add value to the overarching ambition of the organisation or department. Not all measures are KPIs, and not all data collected needs to be used all of the time; refer back to earlier comments regarding the contractual flow-down of Critical Success Factors and contractual Conditions.

When data is collected there is an urge to use it to target or influence an outcome. When targeting, it is essential that the concept of SMART targeting is embraced at all times to make the targeting activity both meaningful and motivating. There also needs to be a diversity in the data to prevent skewing of outcomes and results along with a recognition of the validity of data.

Capture and interpretation of subjective feedback from stakeholders in relation to services is also an important element that is useful to explore in exam responses. Subjective data needs to be assessed and calibrated against a consistent scale, with validity increasing the more responses are received.

Examples of subjective data collection and analysis might include:

- Identifying the number of empty plates returning to a canteen gives a measure of the tastiness of a meal;
- Number of sick days taken (maybe using the Bradford Index) or staff turnover as a subjective measure of staff happiness;
- Data collected from red, amber and green / sad, somber or smiley face buttons in some retail stores or in airport customs.

SMART targets are considered more effective and conducive to achievement and improving performance. These features should therefore be considered whenever setting corporate or personal goals and targets – as well as within exam or assignment settings to highlight the multi-dimensional nature of measurements – see figure x.

- **Specific** - Target needs to be clear and unambiguous
- **Measurable** - Target needs to have a clear measure and an undisputed data source
- **Achievable** - The target must be achievable as otherwise it will demotivate
- **Relevant** - The target must be relevant to the organisation and add some obvious value to its goals
- **Timed** - Target must have a starting point and a finishing point

Figure x – SMART Targets

Note: The SMART model is generally recognised as being thus, however in some circumstances the letters have been adjusted - for example Realistic sometimes replaces Relevant or Attainment instead of Achievable – yet the method and concept remains the same, to effectively set goals and achieve them.

The Finance Department, A Critical Stakeholder

In Procurement and Supply Chain Management, along with other commercial functions in the organisation, there can be a tendency to forget or circumnavigate the Finance function in the day-to-day operational activities.

Whilst to many, the Finance team are the archetypal "Blocker" in the organisation, we must be cognisant of their critical contribution within the Procurement Cycle, and especially with the thorny issue of paying suppliers on time. Admittedly the commercial pressure to delay payment for as long as possible to maximise bank deposit interest has decreased in recent years due to lower interest rates, however the commitments made in negotiations to prompt payment terms are often lost in translation and late payment excused with a missed payment run or similar justification.

Whether answering exam questions, running a project or participating in day-to-day process, awareness of the relationship between the Supplier and the Organisation is essential.

There are normally three points of contact between a Supplier and a Buying Organisation, but when discussing Supplier Relationship Management it is often only the Supplier-Buyer element which is analysed, measured and documented, see figure xi:

Figure xi – Supplier Interaction with the Buying Organisation

Historically, the focus from both the Buyer and the Seller is within the value generating elements of this relationship, i.e. the quotation, order generation and delivery angles, however a focused commercial operative should be ever mindful of efficiency and the elimination of waste within the process.

With this in mind, the generation of quarantined items, commercial queries, debit notes and indeed the associated remedial activity and credit notes is a key area of note in best practice and exams, and one that is often overlooked.

In preparation for any exam, it is worth reviewing some of the Finance elements such as financial structure, cost and profit elements, and the aforementioned payment essentials. Knowledge of ratios is often a good area for bonus marks with ratios grouped in one of three categories: Profitability, Liquidity, Financing.

From a Procurement perspective, we need to take particular interest in these categories and address three core questions:

1. Are we and the Supplier making a fair profit or commercial return;
2. Is the flow of funds between the Buyer and the Supplier and between the Supplier and the Second Tier Supplier healthy, and;
3. What is the nature of the Supplier's funding arrangements and are payments and premiums within acceptable risk parameters?

In terms of financial ratios, the following are recommended starting points to illustrate understanding, shown in figure xii:

Profitability Ratios	Liquidity Ratios	Financing Ratios
• Gross Profit • Mark-Up • Net Margin • EBITDA	• Current Ratio • Quick Ratio • Debtor & Creditor Days • Stock Turnover	• Debt Gearing • Earnings Ratios • Return on Investment

Figure xii – Sample Financial ratios

Useful Everyday Examples In Exam Answers

As mentioned hitherto in the Point-Reason-Example-Model exam question structure, the use of examples in academic answers is a hugely effective way of demonstrating understanding and application of academic learning outcomes, and is often an extremely useful source of marks and reward.

Prior to an exam, ensure that you have identified a broad range of examples to help underpin the key messages in your exam answer. Below are an oft used selection of example case studies along with the areas where they can be of use.

Such examples can be explored using site visits, researched through the internet, or explored using virtual experiences such as YouTube Videos or VidBlinqz:

Amazon: Optimised use of data, Distribution Logistics, warehouse efficiency, innovative delivery solutions;

Toyota: Automotive in general is a useful source showing, JIT processing, efficient production systems, agile design & production, and waste management;

Coffee Shops: Useful analysis of soft commodity, seasonal Supply Chains, management of non-indigenous waste;

Disposal of Waste: Further, Starbucks' and Costa's use of the bean bags as free of charge packaging and free micro disposal of the coffee grounds highlights an efficient and effective disposals solution;

Symbiosis: Brands of Yeast Extract align with local brewers such as Marmite and Marstons Ale; equally consider a hippo & oxpecker;

McDonald's: Is a good example of consistency in a Supply scenario; the image, colours, logos, menu and promotions are consistenty applied across all stores across a region and sometimes globally. The Drive-Thru is also an example of JIT processing;

Domestic Printers: Highlights the concept of Total Cost of Ownership as the price of the printer ink cartridges will heavily outweigh the cost of the printer itself;

Loyalty Cards: Store loyalty cards – and especially those by big supermarkets – are a useful example of the management of big data coupled with bespoke customer deals and special offers;

Supermarkets: Useful to highlight effective use of risk and margin management in a retail setting. Coupled with loyalty cards, both the customer experience and commercial endeavours of the supermarket are aligned;

Store Layout: Optimised use of storage space and careful positioning of product can significantly help with aspects such as stock rotation, management of inventory levels, managing shelf-life or obsolescence management;

Shelf Restocking: Use of IT solutions to trigger replenishment of the shelf with infrastructure such as wheeled cages used as a Kanban Pull solution;
Shipping Totes: Development of bespoke reusable packaging designed to fit snugly in the distribution vehicle optimising space and reduced waiting times through enhancing loading and unloading;

Milkmen: The traditional concept of a milkman is a good example of an agile supply solution, reducing unnecessary inventory using recycled packaging and delivered using an environmentally conscious electrical vehicle;

Supply Agility: Zara, Primark and others display an incredible ability and agility to identify a consumer demand, design, prototype, sign-off and manufacture product in a matter of a few days (typically around 14 days), this compares to many months with traditional retailers;

Lithium Batteries: The development of Lithium battery technology has led to enormous challenges with volatility, thermal events (fires and explosions), transportation, packaging and logistical solutions to name a few, and will play a big role in the transition towards electric vehicles;

Consistency: Focussing on a single connector within the phone market failed to materialise as neither of the main protagonists were willing to adopt the charging connector of the other, though it did eliminate a number of the peripheral connectors. With vehicular battery-charging taking a time, moving to a single interchangeable connector would enable quick and efficient changeover of battery during a journey;

Product Lifecycles: Consider the evolution of the phone market over the years with a steady change in the market leader with the 1990's dominated by organisations such as Motorola rolling forward into Nokia, then Blackberry and onto Apple before Samsung took over as number one in the handset sales. As at the start of 2020, Apple has retained its level of profitability through migrating into the development of the soft and platform side of the business;

Technology: Kodak's decision to focus on cellulose photography rather than digital meant that they fell behind the market in developing cameras that reflected the modern expectation of the consumer, leading ultimately to their demise and failure;

Social Changes: Equally, the demise of Lego can be shown to have been wrested and resurrected with a focus on new, more complicated but exciting parts aligned to other market drivers such as film and computer gaming;

Political Change: Changes in political structures such as the move towards democratisation of the Chinese Republic, the Post-Brexit European Union, and further back the end of Apartheid or the warming of East-West relations after the Cold War, can have dramatic changes in supply and demand in markets;

Legislation: Changes in the prevailing legislation in a legal and economic arena, and wider on a global platform. Such legislation can apply to a huge range of commercial and social facets which can dramatically affect a procurement operation;

Waste Rules: Aligned with the legislation, the WEEE Regulations govern the management of waste materials arising from all things electronic or electrical and is an easy example of environmental legislation;

Employment Regulations: The Modern Slavery Act, the Ethical Trade Initiative, TUPE and Working Time Directives are good examples of ethical employment;

Ethical Issues: Manufacture of Lithium batteries utilises a notable quantity of Cobalt, the main producer of which is the Democratic Republic of Congo, a country with an historic record of child and slave labour.

Student Exam Guidance

Be Aware Of ISO Standards & Legislation

In addition to using examples to substantiate a point, understanding some of the key ISO standards can be useful to illustrate a deeper understanding of a particular situation; some of the main ISO standards used within a Procurement & Supply Chain situation are as follows:

- **ISO9000**   Quality Management
- **ISO14000**   Environmental Management
- **ISO18000**   HSE Management
- **ISO26000**   Social Responsibility
- **ISO27000**   IT Security
- **ISO31000**   Risk Management

Further, building on earlier comments regarding legal matters, being able to cite some key elements of legislation is often rewarded in exam marking structures. For example, referencing WTO rulings, European Directives, US constitutional elements or UK law is worth considering; below are a few examples correct at the time of print:

- WTO Vienna Convention on the Law of Treaties
- EU Health & Safety Framework Directive
- UK Consumer Rights Act
- US transparency in Negotiation Act (TINA)
- EU Rotterdam Rules on International Transportation of Goods
- EU Waste Electrical and Electronic Equipment (WEEE) Regulations
- ILO Conventions on Child Labour
- US Fair Labor Standards Act (FLSA)
- EU Treaty of Europe

Procurement & Supply Chain Management Models

Business Analysis
1. Ansoff Planning Model
2. Balanced Scorecards
3. Critical Needs Analysis (CNA)
4. Pareto Analysis
5. PEST / PESTLE / STEEPLE / STEEPLED Analysis
6. SWOT Analysis & TOWS Strategy Model

Category Management
7. AT Kearney Seven Step Category Management Model
8. Bartolini Scorecard
9. CIPS Category Management Model
10. Jackson & Crocker Category Management Model
11. OSCAR Model

Contract & Change Management
12. ADR
13. Carter 6S Contract Management Model
14. Kotter 8 Phases of Change
15. Lewin Freeze & Force Field Analysis Models
16. Parker Supplier Performance Review (SUPER) Model

Cost & Value
17. Activity Based Costing
18. Kano model
19. Porter Value Chain
20. Total Cost of Ownership Model
21. Value Analysis & Value Stream Mapping

Ethical & Environmental
22. 8R Model of Responsible Waste Treatment
23. 4D Model
24. Green Diversity Model

25. Inequality -Types and Principles
26. Nine Dimensions of Sustainability
27. Ohno Seven Wastes
28. 3E Model
29. 3i Model

Human Resource Management
30. Belbin Team Roles
31. Crocker Triangle
32. Eysenck Hierarchical Model of Personality
33. Goleman's Domains of Emotional Intelligence
34. Hofstede Cultural Factors Model
35. Honey & Mumford Learning Styles
36. HR RITUAL
37. Johnson Cultural Web
38. RACI Assessment
39. Rodgers Seven Point Plan
40. Training Needs Analysis - Vanguard Model

Management & Leadership
41. Adair Action-Centred Leadership Model
42. Ashridge Management Styles
43. Cialdini Six Principles of Persuasion
44. Fayol Principles of Management
45. Greiner Growth Model
46. Hersey-Blanchard Model
47. Herzberg Hygiene/Motivators
48. Hierarchy of Objectives
49. Maslow Hierarchy of Needs
50. McKinsey 7S Model
51. Mintzberg 5P Model
52. Mintzberg Management Roles
53. Mullins Process of Management Model
54. Nadler and Tushman Congruence Model
55. Organisational Balance Model
56. Senge Five Disciplines
57. Theory X, Theory Y and Theory Z
58. Trait Theory

59. Trist & Bamforth Socio-Technical Approach
60. Tuckman Team Development

Market & Price Analysis
61. Ansoff Matrix
62. Boston Consulting Group Matrix & PLC
63. Kotler 4P Model
64. Porter Competitive Advantage Model
65. Porter Five Force Model
66. Supply Market Analysis

Procurement
67. Carter 10C Model
68. Crocker Simplified Service Gap Model
69. Five Rights of Purchasing
70. Iron Triangle Model
71. Kraljic Matrix
72. Maturity Assessment Model
73. Monczka MSU Model
74. Steele & Court Supplier Preferencing Model
75. Syson Positioning Graph - Strategic Policies
74a Syson Positioning Graph - Strategic Performance

Quality
76. Cost of Poor Quality (COPQ) Model
77. Deming / Shewhart Plan-Do-Check-Act (PDCA)
78. EFQM Excellence Model
79. Fishbone / Root Cause Analysis / Ishikawa Diagram
80. Kaizen
81. Six Sigma, DMAIC & SIPOC Models
82. Voice of the Customer & Quality Circles

Relationships & Stakeholder Management
83. Burnes & New Customer/Supplier Relationships
84. Cox Supplier Relationships Management Model
85. Crocker Managing Satisfaction of Service Quality Model
86. Customer-Supplier Partnership Bridge
87. Egan Stakeholder Positioning (Labels) Model

88. Johnson Supplier Management Behaviours Model
89. Mendelow Matrix
90. Relationship Determination Model
91. Stakeholder Allegiance Matrix
92. Supplier Relationship Management (SRM) Interfaces
93. Thomas & Kilmann Conflict Mode Instrument

Risk
94. Business Continuity Planning
95. Four T Model of Risk
96. Risk Cycle
97. Risk-Impact Model

Strategic Supply Chain Management
98. Bhattacharya Outsourcing Decision Model
99. Christopher & Towill Lean Agile Matrix
100. Cousins Strategic Supply Wheel
101. Goldratt Theory of Constraints
102. Inventory Decision Matrix

Business Analysis

1. Ansoff Planning Model
2. Balanced Scorecards
3. Critical Needs Analysis (CNA)
4. Pareto Analysis
5. PEST / PESTLE / STEEPLE / STEEPLED Analysis
6. SWOT Analysis & TOWS Strategy Model

102 Models of Procurement & Supply Chain Management

1. Ansoff Planning Model

The Ansoff Planning Model is used to identify planning requirements and process within an organisation as well as establishing review and monitoring process to enable improved control of the business activities – remember, if you can't measure it, you can't manage it!

The Ansoff Planning Model steps through the managerial planning process, through the initial stages of analysis, to identifying opportunity, selection of options, final decision making and implementation.

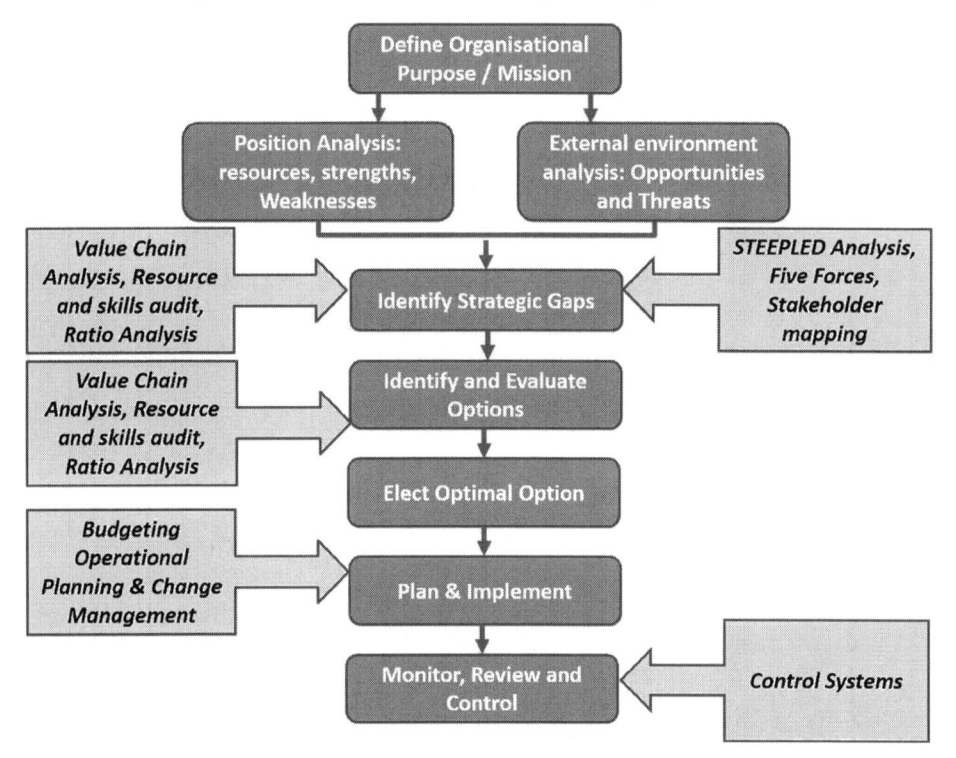

```
                    Define Organisational
                      Purpose / Mission
                              |
            ┌─────────────────┴─────────────────┐
      Position Analysis:              External environment
    resources, strengths,           analysis: Opportunities
       Weaknesses                         and Threats

  Value Chain                                          STEEPLED Analysis,
  Analysis, Resource                                   Five Forces,
  and skills audit,    →   Identify Strategic Gaps  ←  Stakeholder
  Ratio Analysis                                       mapping

  Value Chain
  Analysis, Resource       Identify and Evaluate
  and skills audit,    →         Options
  Ratio Analysis

                            Elect Optimal Option

  Budgeting
  Operational
  Planning & Change    →    Plan & Implement
  Management

                          Monitor, Review and   ←   Control Systems
                                Control
```

The model incorporates the critical review and feedback loops and can also use the other major models to generate inputs throughout as shown.

Positive Views on Model	Negative Views on Model
• Draws models into the planning process • Generates a clear end product	• Often difficult for practitioners to associate with

32

2. Balanced Scorecards

The Kaplan and Norton(1992) Balanced Scorecard is a robust and structured report underpinned with well–established processes and methods. It is used by organisations to measure, manage and verify performance across a number of core business facets.

The Balanced Scorecard was conceived by Robert Kaplan and David Norton with a focus on developing performance measures that are based on aspects other than just financial return. These additional measures include analysis of the success of customer interaction, the effectiveness and suitability of internal business processes, and how it treats and utilises its employees.

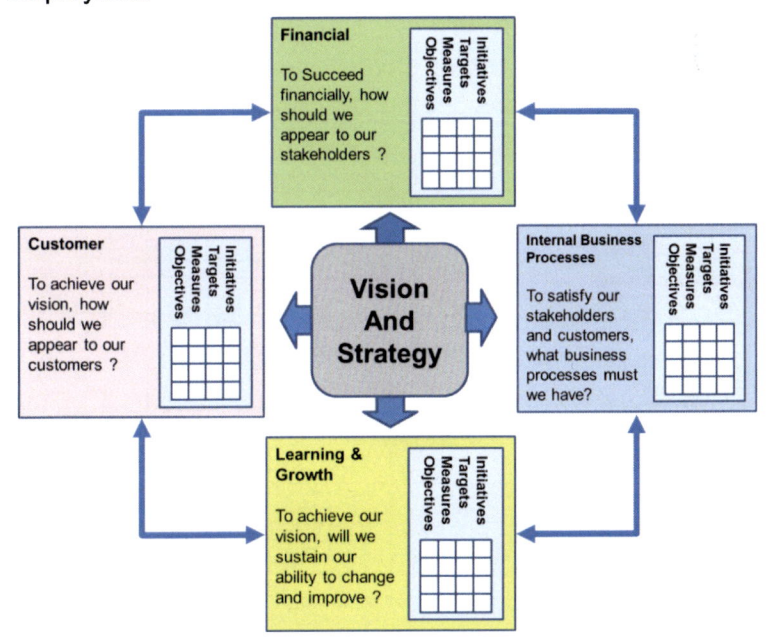

Financial
To Succeed financially, how should we appear to our stakeholders?

Customer
To achieve our vision, how should we appear to our customers?

Internal Business Processes
To satisfy our stakeholders and customers, what business processes must we have?

Learning & Growth
To achieve our vision, will we sustain our ability to change and improve?

Vision And Strategy

Each perspective includes: Initiatives, Targets, Measures, Objectives.

These four aspects form the basis of the model and highlight what should be measured and managed, with assessments of targets and objectives.

Positive Views on Model	Negative Views on Model
• Gives an overall view of the health of the organisation • Flexible to suit the specific needs of the business	• May distract from the financial requirements • Can be difficult to create the specific metrics required especially if they're subjective

3. Critical Needs Analysis (CNA)

Critical Needs Analysis is used to determine the critical features necessary for the supply or production of an item or service to ensure it has all necessary features yet is not over engineered or gold plated. The item or service shall endeavour to be just "Fit for Purpose".

In a Critical Needs Analysis evaluation, all the needs are listed and categorised as either primary functions or secondary functions, no other features will then affect the determination of the chosen solution. The approach needs a cross–functional methodology to avoid a skewed perspective and should maintain a non–supplier specific perspective. This process should be used as a forerunner to the production of a specification so demands a diverse stakeholder input and should not – especially in a public sector environment – involve any supplier involvement. For example consider the selection of a writing implement.

	Primary Needs			Secondary Needs				
Score 1-5 weighed x2 for primary factors and x1 for secondary factors.	Cost	Cost of Ink	Quality of ink	Flexibility	Leakage	Versatility	Ergonomics	Transportable	Totals
Ball Point Pen	4	4	2	4	4	5	3	4	44
Fountain Pen	1	3	5	4	2	3	4	3	38
Roller Ball Pen	3	4	4	5	4	3	3	3	45
Fibre Tip	4	2	2	3	5	3	2	4	36
Pencil	5	5	1	3	5	3	3	5	44
Feather Quill	1	3	3	1	5	1	1	2	25

Positive Views on Model	Negative Views on Model
• Drives the inclusion of only "Value Added" aspects of a design • Allows the Weighting of options • Enables prioritisation of needs	• Needs diverse input to be effective • Ignores other needs that may evolve • May not appreciate all the options leading to possible idea stagnation

4. Pareto Analysis

Pareto Analysis, often known as the 80:20 rule, suggests that 80% of the outcome will come from 20% of the causes. This can be shown using empirical analysis and is a phenomenon commonly seen in nature.

The Pareto or 80:20 rule is a commonly referred to concept in business, mathematics, economics, as well as many sciences and in nature. It suggests that 80% of an output will come from 20% of the inputs, for example, 80% of sales will come from 20% of the customers, 80% of the deliveries will come from 20% of the inventory, 80% of accidents will be attributed to just 20% of the risks.

The Pareto Principle can be explained mathematically (Reference Power Law Distribution Concept model outside the scope of this book), but was originally identified through observation of natural occurrences such as 80% of land in Italy was owned by 20% of the population, 80% of a crop will come from 20% of the seed and 80% of wealth comes from 20% of the population. In business, the Pareto concept is seen regularly where statistical analysis is used, for example, inventory management activities, Six Sigma, in Activity Based Costing models, forecasting and projection models.

In inventory, it is used alongside other concepts – for example the Normal Distribution – to help eliminate dead or excess stock, to improve service levels, plan warehouse locations, and assign inventory categories. In a customer facing warehouse for example, fast moving A stock (the top 20% of products which will account for 80% of the sales and thus 80% of the stock picks) should be located nearest to the sales counter to help reduce customer waiting time, and sales staff distance travelled to pick an item.

Positive Views on Model	Negative Views on Model
• Well established natural occurrence • Used in many statistical applications across the business	• Doesn't work well with low numbers of inputs or outputs • Rarely exactly 80% so needs to still be calculated • Other models exist such as Theil index

5. PEST / PESTLE / STEEPLE / STEEPLED Analysis

The PEST, PESTLE, STEEPLE and STEEPLED acronym models are used to assess the external environment in which the organisation operates. PEST (Political, Economic, Social, Technical) was the original model but grew to form PESTLE (with Legislation and Environmental) which has, itself, grown in recent times to indicate Ethical factors giving an extra E and a D for Demographics making the word STEEPLED.

The STEEPLED model looks at the external aspects that can affect an organisation. These include:

S – Social Factors – People and community issues such as the standard of living, welfare, happiness;
T – Technical Factors – The level of technology in the market, technical complexity of product and components, or software issues;
E – Economic Factors – These may include aspects such as the value of currency, GDP rates, minimum wage, debt levels, or unemployment;
E – Environmental Factors – These relate to issues with aspects like climate change, global warming, use of resources and pollution;
P – Political Factors – May include aspects such as a change in government or political ethos, electorate swings, or dominant leaders;
L – Legislation – Will address changes in laws, trade restrictions, the position taken by the judiciary and determinations made in court;
E – Ethical Issues – including corruption, extortion, bribery, collusion, dubious sources of finance, and reducing child labour and slavery;
D – Demographical Issues – such as size and make–up of population, education levels, religion, gender split, and behaviours of the people.

This model encourages thorough consideration of external aspects that could affect the organisation both positively and negatively.

Positive Views on Model	Negative Views on Model
• Simple but internationally recognised acronym checklist • Useful checklist for someone considering external factors	• Model has evolved but many still use PEST/PESTLE and do not recognise SLEPT, STEEPLE or STEEPLED

6. SWOT Analysis & TOWS Strategy Model

A SWOT Analysis is used to assess the internal capabilities of an organisation to understand its ability to perform in a particular scenario. The TOWS model was a later extension to the SWOT model which sought to generate or drive the formulation of a strategy from the SWOT findings.

The SWOT Analysis was developed by the Stanford Research Institute is used to analyse the capabilities of an organisation to compete and capitalise on corporate opportunities. It is used to identify an organisation's strengths, weaknesses, opportunities and threats:

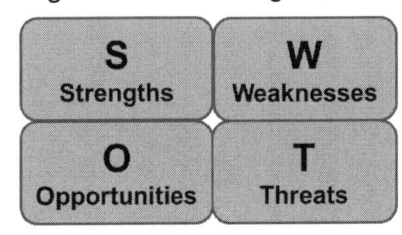

S Strengths	**W** Weaknesses
O Opportunities	**T** Threats

The TOWS model goes further turning the SWOT Analysis into a functional strategy development tool that reflects issues and actions required associated with each intersect:

	Opportunities External Positive Impacts	Threats External Negative Impacts
Strengths Internal Positive Impacts	Utilise the strengths in the most effective way to capitalise upon the opportunities	Utilise the strengths of the organisation to combat against and minimise the impact of the threats
Weaknesses Internal Negative Impacts	Address the weaknesses in the organisation that prevent it from capitalising on the opportunities	Create strategy to minimise the organisation's weaknesses to protect it against the threats

Positive Views on Model	Negative Views on Model
- SWOT model widely recognised and commonly used model - Easy to understand and implement	- SWOT does not deliver a clear strategy - TOWS relatively unknown and used less than SWOT

Category Management

7. AT Kearney Seven Step Category Management Model
8. Bartolini Scorecard
9. CIPS Category Management Model
10. Jackson & Crocker Category Management Model
11. OSCAR Model

7. AT Kearney Seven Step Category Management Model

The AT Kearney Seven Step Category Management Model is a well-recognised Category Management solution running from the initial profiling activity through to the ongoing benchmarking of the Category against the marketplace as a whole.

The AT Kearney Model was developed in 2001 to take the Category Management concept into a new era.

The approach was primarily focused on the reduction in cost, although the profiling activity does ensure category completeness and sourcing strategy.

| 1. Profile the Category | 2. Select Sourcing Strategy | 3. Generate Supplier Portfolio | 4. Select Implementation Path | 5. Negotiate & Select Suppliers | 6. Integrate Suppliers | 7. Benchmark Supply Market |

The process begins, as with a number of the Category Management solutions, with the organising of the category profile before determining the optimum sourcing solution(s) to be adopted for the profile. As part of this sourcing strategy, maintenance, negotiation and development of the supplier base and selection process is essential to ensure the correct suppliers are in place to deliver the optimum stakeholder service. Once agreed, the process also considers how the solutions are integrated through effective project implementation with the Category Management solutions and dovetailed with the existing options.

Finally, once integrated and running, the AT Kearney approach ensures a continuous evaluation and benchmarking process is in place to maintain the performance and output of the system.

Positive Views on Model	Negative Views on Model
• Succinct solution with steps covering the core areas of Category Management • Recognises the importance of an effective integration	• A lack of a clear adjustment loop limits the ability to adjust and morph systems • Doesn't consider the people side of a Category solution

8. Bartolini Scorecard

The Bartolini Scorecard is used in Category Management to evaluate the suitability and potential viability of a procurement category, enabling categories to be prioritised and resources allocated within the set-up process.

Using a structured questionnaire, the Bartolini scorecard collects relevant data pertaining to a category, evaluates its potential and scores the category accordingly. This detail can then be used to 1) prioritise categories, 2) allocate resources including finance, personnel and time allocation, and 3) identify commercial potential from the category. The model identifies 5 categories against which it evaluates the category – these are:

i. Category specific issues – Aspects relating to the goods and services or collective product segment, for example complexity of the product or lead-time for delivery;

ii. Procurement facets – Consideration of the procurement process, risk analysis, desired outcomes, specifications and stakeholders;

iii. Internal and organisational facets – The structure of the organisation, for example its history, geography, management hierarchy, culture, stakeholder engagement and expectations;

iv. Market facets – Based on the Porter Five Force model, this looks at forces and dynamics in the market, buyers, sellers, barriers to entry, new entrants and alternative solutions;

v. Supplier facets – Finally the model looks at the supplier base, considering aspects such as its competitive nature, prevailing margins, perceived saving opportunity, as well as the type of suppliers, their organisational structure, whether the product is bespoke or generic, design and specification commitment, volume, and spend potential.

Positive Views on Model	Negative Views on Model
• Structured method of evaluation against a clear set of criteria • Enables supplier comparison • Enables resource allocation	• Fixed evaluation criteria • One of several similar models in existence

9. CIPS Category Management Model

The CIPS Category Management Model is a four-phase/six-step process which manages the development and operational delivery of a Category Management solution through operational delivery and review.

The CIPS Category Management Model is a well-established four-phase Category Management process. The Category Management process begins by kicking off the initiative, before Preparing then Delivering the Strategy designed to deliver demonstrable benefit into the Organisation. Finally, as with any initiative, the CIPS model incorporates a feedback and adjustment phase to ensure a Continuous Improvement focus.

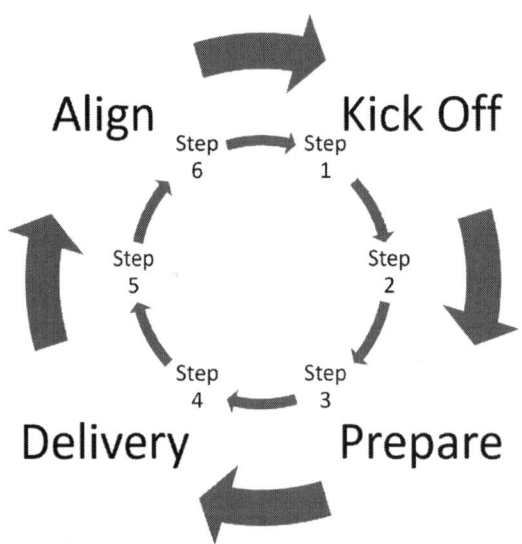

Inside the outer cycle are however 6 other steps which look at the practical delivery of the four primary steps throughout the process.

These inner steps break the four primary phases and are focused on delivery of the bottom-line benefits outlined in the commercial business case.

One criticism of this model is that the diagram fails to clearly delineate between the phases and steps, and that alignment cycles back into the kick-off phase suggesting endless undermining of the initial delivery activity.

Positive Views on Model	Negative Views on Model
• Good step by step process with a clear review mechanism	• Lack of clarity between where phases and steps start and finish in practical terms

Category Management

10. Jackson & Crocker Category Management Model

The Jackson & Crocker Category Management Model was created as a constructive amalgam of the historic category management approaches, incorporating the strengths and focuses of each in a consolidated approach, updating the concepts to reflect the commercial needs of 2020 and beyond.

The Jackson-Crocker Model was built from the successful elements of historic Category Management models which for whatever reason had not evolved with the market or academic developments over the years.

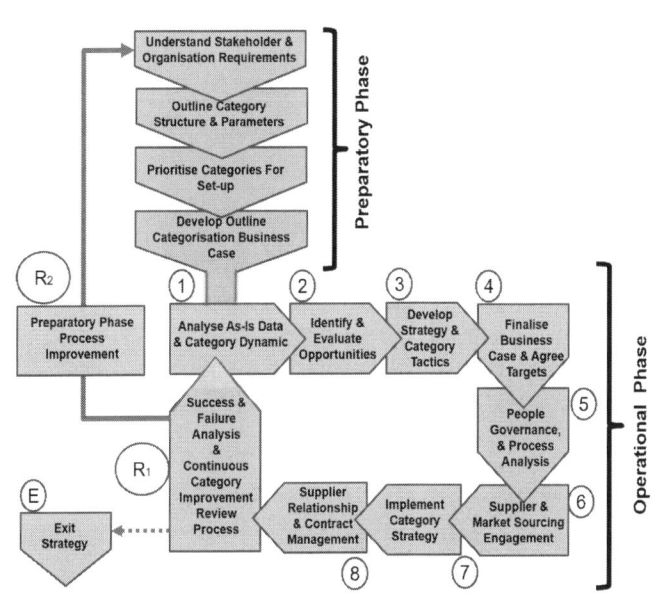

The model suggests that a process needs to have a solid base upon which the delivery of value is generated however this must also recognise that the environment in which the system sits is liable to reactive change as well as more substantial long-term evolution.

Whilst there are a significant number of steps in the model, each step is based on the successes and omissions from other models and is designed systematically to deliver the operational objectives of quality, time and cost, within a balanced and sustainable, risk free environment.

Positive Views on Model	Negative Views on Model
• Incorporates positive elements from historic models as well as a commercial closure option to enable termination if required	• A large number of steps may make this difficult for operational members to follow

11. OSCAR Model

The OSCAR model is a simple acronym generated to help remind students of the five core values generated from an effective Category Management process namely: Outsourcing non-core elements, Standardisation; Categorisation; Aggregation; and Relationships.

The acronym is intended to remind students and practitioners of the values generated in a Category Management solution.

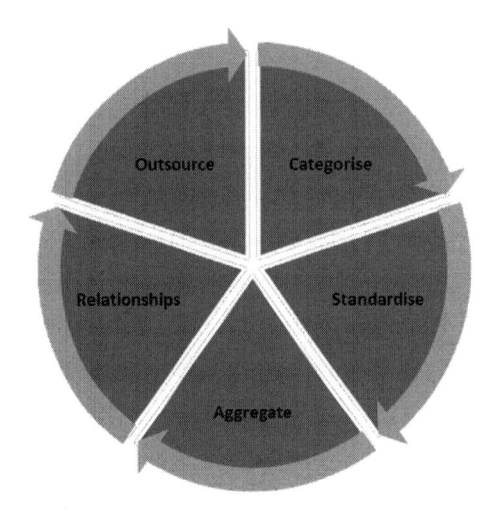

Step 1 – Categorise Sort out the profile of goods or services in the Category

Step 2 – Standardise With Stakeholder input, standardise and simplify the profile

Step 3 – Aggregate Spend Reduce the number of suppliers generate Leverage

Step 4 – Relationships Build stronger relationships with a reduced Supplier base

Step 5 – Outsource Focus on the strategic elements of the profile that add most value

In essence, the process of a Category Management function has five clear commercial steps, with each step having a demonstrable benefit to the commercial bottom-line. Whilst the letters in the acronym are not in a logical sequence the word OSCAR serves as an aide-memoire especially in the stresses of an exam scenario.

Positive Views on Model	Negative Views on Model
• Simplistic focus on commercial benefits generated from a Category Solution • Useful *aide-memoire* for students in exams	• Ignores some of the other elements of Category Management addressed by other models

Contract & Change Management

12. ADR Alternative Dispute Resolution
13. Carter 6S Contract Management Model
14. Kotter 8 Phases of Change
15. Lewin Freeze & Force Field Analysis Models
16. Parker Supplier Performance Review (SuPeR) Model

12. ADR Alternative Dispute Resolution

Alternative Dispute Resolution (ADR) is an approach intended to manage contractual disputes with structured options to be used by the contractual parties to help them avoid Litigation.

Alternative Dispute Resolution is a formal and structured approach to encourage contractual parties looking to resolve a dispute through the use of 1) Negotiation, 2) Mediation, 3) Conciliation and 4) Arbitration, though there are various other terms and definitions of the process in some circles.

Whilst this approach gained prominence from the 1980s, it was only introduced into EU law through the European Mediation Directive 2008 and covered disputes where one or more of the parties was domiciled in the EU. The UK has however already made preparations to rescind the Directive following Brexit with an Act of Parliament after EU-Exit Day.

In summary, Negotiation is the first step where the contractual parties try and resolve the issues in private between themselves and without intervention. As the process continues so the level of involvement increases, first with an independent Mediation facilitating the process, then with guidance on a solution through Conciliation, before a firmer solution through Arbitration is determined.

Introducing alternative methods of resolving a dispute is intended to have three core benefits: firstly to enable the parties to resolve the issue quickly and resume their focus on commercial matters; secondly, it removes a large level of cost, time and stress from a commercial disagreement; and thirdly, it helps free up court time for more pressing matters.

Positive Views on Model	Negative Views on Model
• Reduces cost, time and stress • Frees up Court Time	• Can delay the inevitable litigation process • Reveals the other party's position and evidence

13. Carter 6S Contract Management Model

The Carter 6S Contract Management Model is a robust six step contract management process, designed to ensure there is a clear statement of "what success looks like", show what makes a delighted customer and address how to manage and mitigate the risks associated with the project.

The Carter 6S Contract Management Model recognises the need for a clearly defined basis for the contract performance. It starts with ensuring that there is an unambiguous definition of what success would look like.

The six steps are as follows:

Step 1 - Success Supplier and Buyer need to define what is meant by success. Without having a clear idea of what is required and how it will be attained, failure is more likely to occur.

Step 2 - Stakeholder Engagement Supplier and Buyer need to discuss and liaise with the Customer to ensure alignment of ideas or clear participation in the Supply Chain.

Step 3 - Shared Vision Supplier and Buyer need to discuss the requirements and seek a clear and united vision of what is required.

Step 4 - Specification Critical to success is that both Supplier and Buyer have an appropriate specification or scope of work to guide the contractors to ensure the output of goods or services meets Customer expectations.

Step 5 - Strategy A robust, structured and coherent contracting strategy is required to make the contract come to life. For example, this strategy needs to consider cost, value, quality, CSR issues and risk.

Step 6 - Suitable Contract Finally, there is a need for the right type of contract, supported by a robust contract management system to guarantee as far as is possible, that output meets design and customer expectations.

Positive Views on Model	Negative Views on Model
• Model clearly addresses core issues in contract development • Model recognises the issues that cause problems in contract management	• Could look deeper at the evolution of requirements over the contract life

14. Kotter 8 Phases of Change

The Kotter 8 Phases model considers change in 8 steps from the start through to making the change permanent.

The Kotter model breaks the process of change into 8 steps or phases from the initial preparation for work through to the difficult matter of making the change "stick".

The Kotter model begins by generating momentum with stakeholders, before building coalitions to ensure support from key areas. The project must have a clear vision around which stakeholders can unite with this vision and other key components effectively communicated. Once this is in place, delivery commences with a good project manager looking for quick wins to cement support and gather a momentum to the end of the project, with efforts at the conclusion to prevent reversion to the "old ways".

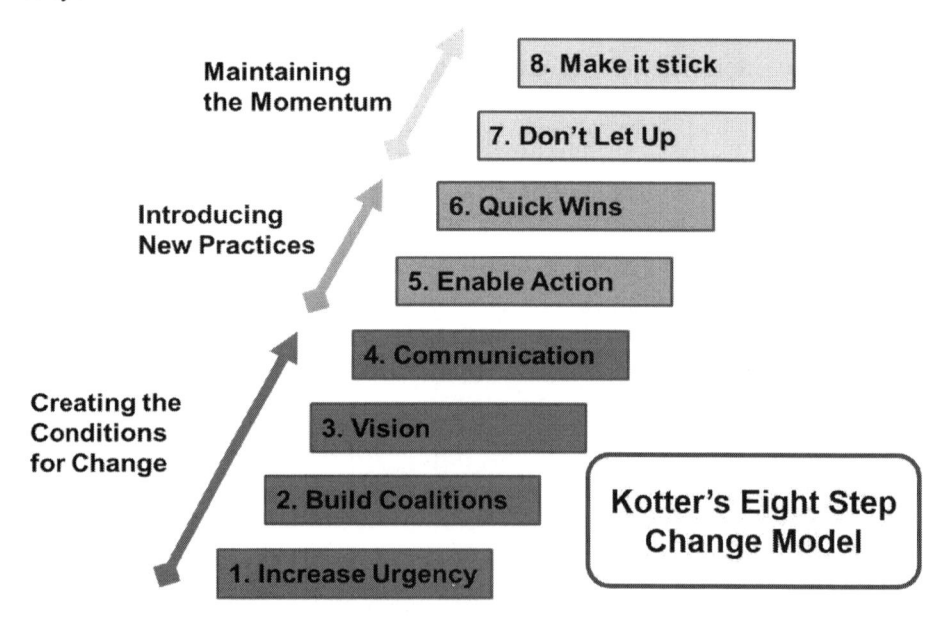

Kotter's Eight Step Change Model

Maintaining the Momentum:
- 8. Make it stick
- 7. Don't Let Up

Introducing New Practices:
- 6. Quick Wins
- 5. Enable Action

Creating the Conditions for Change:
- 4. Communication
- 3. Vision
- 2. Build Coalitions
- 1. Increase Urgency

Positive Views on Model	Negative Views on Model
• Good systematic approach that increases success	• Needs management support and strong leadership
• Reduces the oft inevitable resistance to change	• Being a systematic process it's not very flexible

15. Lewin Freeze & Force Field Analysis Models

The Lewin Freeze and Force Field Models firstly identify the need to unfreeze a situation before effective change can be implemented remembering to refreeze it afterwards to embed the change, but secondly, alongside there needs to be a focus on all the forces acting on the project, both those in favour and those against, these assessed using the Force Field Analysis.

The Freeze Model is used to modify behaviours through unfreezing the activity or process, implementing the change and then refreezing to cement the change introduced. Implementing change without the necessary preparation and "warming" of the team, merely leads to anguish and stress, the change fails to break the habit, and reversion to the old processes is then often inevitable. Organisations, and more importantly the individuals therein, need to be aware of the change, be enlightened as to the reasons and benefits of the change, and have a clearly identified pathway or project plan. Once implemented, the amended system, process or structure needs to be refrozen, made the formal practice and embedded in the organisation's modus operandi with amendments made to the organisations operating procedures and process manual where necessary.

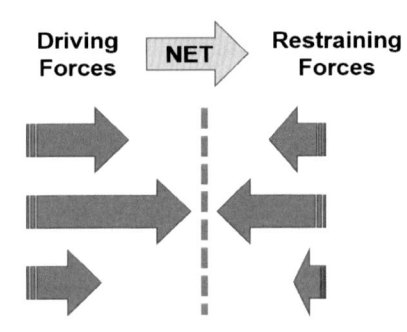

Attention should also be paid to the Force Field of positive and negative opinion to a project. To ensure progress, the positive forces will need to outweigh those against the project and Lewin's Force Field Analysis assesses these respective forces to ensure a net support is positive.

Note however, Nadler and Tushman suggested that different approaches for delivering change are required in different scenarios.

Positive Views on Model	Negative Views on Model
• Simple model with clear objectives and process • Shows the importance of the need to embed change	• Some would argue it's merely a common sense approach to warm the people who will be affected by the change.

16. Parker Supplier Performance Review SuPeR Model

The Parker Supplier Performance Review Model (SuPeR) is designed to enable buyers to quickly and easily review Supplier performance giving an anonymous visual benchmarked of performance relative to value to help highlight the supplier's shortcomings.

The Parker Supplier Performance Review (SuPeR) Model generates a visual comparison of the performance of a supplier based on On-Time-In-Full (OTIF) delivery, but recognising the relative value of the Supplier's account to the Buying organisation. Colour coded using traffic-light protocols, this enables the Buyer to quickly identify where the poor performing suppliers are situated and thus take remedial actions.

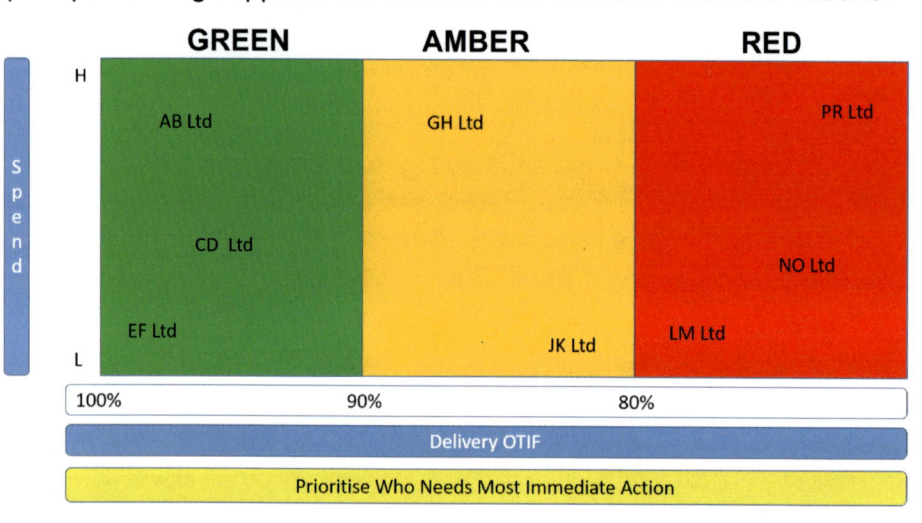

Whilst the parameters in the model can be adjusted to reflect an organisation's specific requirements, initial recommendations are given as:
- The Green zone is acceptable performance (90-100% Del OTIF)
- The Amber zone signals needs improvement (80-90% Del OTIF)
- The Red zone means unacceptable supplier performance (<80%)

Positive Views on Model	Negative Views on Model
• Good conceptual model with clear colour coded output • Gives supplier detail in a useful benchmarked format	• Model doesn't address the relative risk levels of each supplier nor how they view the buying organisation in terms of attractiveness

Cost & Value

17. Activity Based Costing
18. Kano model
19. Porter Value Chain
20. Total Cost of Ownership Model
21. Value Analysis & Value Stream Mapping

17. Activity Based Costing

Activity Based Costing looks at how cost can be allocated within a business based on usage or some other activity. When implemented, this gives a fairer, more strategic and manageable allocation of cost across a business.

The concept of Activity Based Costing (ABC) has evolved over the years to enable organisations to allocate costs more strategically within business units, through geographic locations, by product or simply by usage. This concept is liked by accountants and managers who feel they do not get value for money from corporate overheads, and has developed significantly since usage data has become easier and cheaper to track using IT solutions along with data capture from advances like swipe cards, coded access on equipment such as photocopiers, or vehicle tracking systems amongst others. Allocation can be via a number of options including:

- Equitable Allocation – Cost is distributed equally across the stakeholder groups irrespective of usage. Easy to calculate but penalises those who do not use the goods or services;
- Allocation by usage – Cost is allocated pro rata to usage, however it can be difficult and costly to directly attribute usage, and can result in internal conflict between departments;
- Allocation by sales – Cost is allocated to department in relation to the level of sales contributed. Assumes that a department with a large sales contribution will have a corresponding ability to contribute;
- Allocation by Geography – Cost is allocated based on geography, i.e. if the cost was consumed in Italy it would be allocated to the Italian business. Can cause national or regional resentment and increases risk of exploitation of different tax regimes;
- Allocation by Product – Cost is allocated based on the product within the organisation's portfolio to which it relates.

Positive Views on Model	Negative Views on Model
• Improves management of costs • Increases visibility and ownership • Brings budget and behaviour closer together	• Data capture can be an issue • Selection of the allocation method can cause problems • Workers start to hide usage

18. Kano Model

The Kano model is used in Value Engineering as a systematic approach to enhancing the value of a project by seeking optimal design solutions, thereby reducing unnecessary cost, whilst maintaining and enhancing all aspects of quality and function.

The Kano Model (1984) is a systematic process for improving the value of a new product, service or project, used to:

- Determine the value generated by each component used;
- Identify cost reduction opportunities across the production process;
- Define what constitutes "value", how it can be improved;
- Identify and analyse cost through 'cost targeting':
  - Decide on selling price the market will accept;
  - Decide the minimum profit level acceptable;
  - Identify aspirational target price.

This is a model to decide which functions a new product or service should have and it has the following 5 types of requirements:

Requirements	Explanation
Attractive Requirements	If product/service meets these requirements, it is more likely to attract more customers and create differentiation from rivals
One-Dimensional or Performance Requirements	The more requirements meet customer's needs, with higher level of performance, the more satisfied a customer will be.
Mandatory requirements	Customers definitely want these and will be dissatisfied if they are not present.
Indifferent requirements	These are of little or no relevance to the customer and thus don't influence selection of the product.
Reverse Requirements	These are perceived negatively and so have a reverse effect.

Positive Views on Model	Negative Views on Model
• Helps to deliver functions that delight customers and go beyond expectations without adding undue costs	• Care should be taken evaluating customers responses

19. Porter Value Chain

The Porter Value Chain can be used to identify where in an organisation's business activities it generates value. The Value Chain splits the organisation into Primary and Secondary business facets enabling the analyst to evaluate more precisely the value contribution of each element.

The Porter Value Chain(1985) segments the organisation's operational activities into Primary and Secondary operations allowing the value attained from each to be quantified and understood. The value can be evaluated in various ways – for example financial contribution, time saved or quality improved – and strategy can be adopted to improve the value generated in each. It is common to use this model in conjunction with others, for example a SWOT/TOWS Analysis or STEEPLED Analysis to enable tangible outcomes and deliverables to be established.

The model also recognises that some functions such as Procurement or HR transcend the organisation, adding specific value, and highlight that a unified and consistent strategy helps add value here also allowing critical points in an organisation's business activities to be identified.

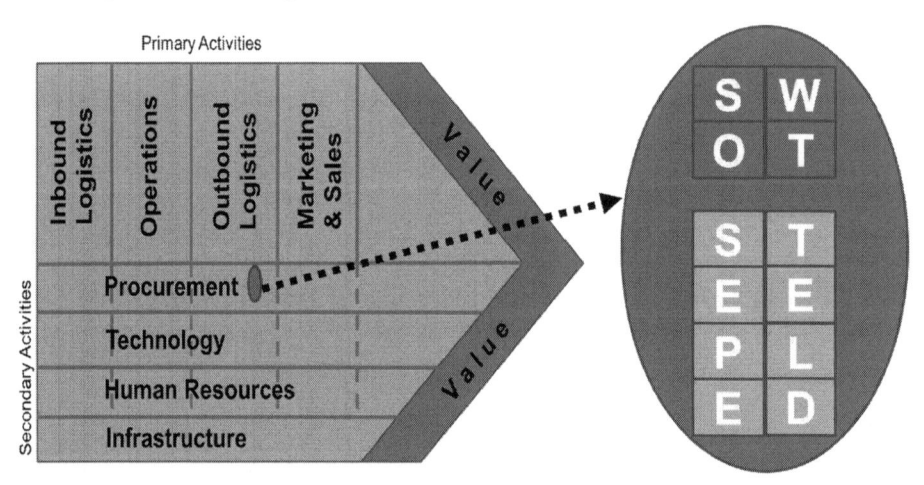

Positive Views on Model	Negative Views on Model
• Long-established model • Can be adapted to include numbers and magnitude	• Understanding of the model often poor and can be difficult to populate with numbers • Product not service orientated

20. Total Cost of Ownership Model

The Total Cost of Ownership Model considers all the costs associated with a purchase as opposed to just the purchase price. This gives a far better reflection of what a purchase may cost in totality over its operational life.

The Total Cost of Ownership Model identifies the core elements of costs to be considered when determining the "best solution". It's not just the invoice price, but the pre-purchase research and dialogue, the preparation of the business case, the tender process and the meetings as well as the after costs associated with the purchase, such as the maintenance, upgrades, repairs, durables, training, security, product support and technical backup. This can be seen illustrated by the Total Cost Iceberg (Bailey, Farmer, Crocker et al 2015) below.

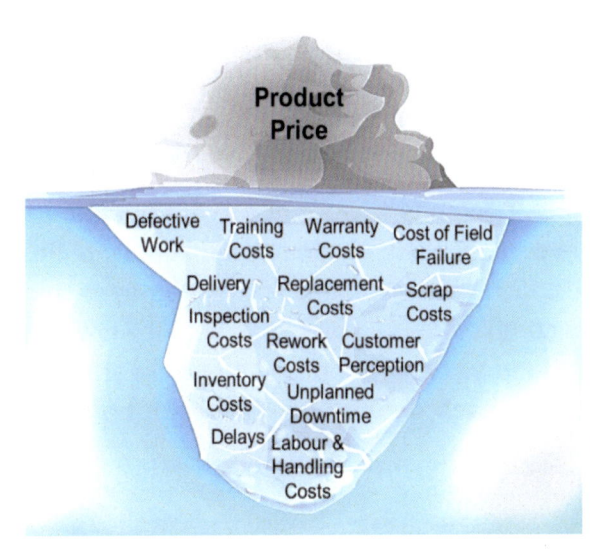

Consider a domestic computer printer: The printer itself is often very cheap compared to the cost of just one ink cartridge that goes in it.

You also need to remember the disposal costs with the TCO model, an area often covered by legislation such at the WEEE rules.

Positive Views on Model	Negative Views on Model
• Clearly illustrates all the costs that make up the Total Cost • Iceberg analogue easy to understand and associate with	• Needs knowledgeable user to be able to recognise all the associated costs even non-recurring or one-off costs

21. Value Analysis & Value Stream Mapping

Value Analysis is a structured process that aims to ensure the production process delivers all the elements of the specification and aspirations of the Stakeholders at the lowest Total Cost of Ownership. Value Stream mapping identifies where in the process the Value is generated.

The concept of Value Analysis is often introduced as a process which looks to understand the costs involved with a production process, stripping out any cost which does not add value within the overall production schemes; if it doesn't add positively to the end goal, the final solution, and can be removed without detriment, it is removed. The removal must not restrict performance, damage quality, or in any way reduce the benefit to the user.

In contrast Value Stream Mapping looks at where in a process value is added. It looks at how effort, time and process change the total value of the components into something of greater worth. As an example, consider a block of stone. A sculptor starts chipping, each hammer blow creates value as the rock becomes a work of art, the final piece being more valuable than the original block. Once formed in outline, the sculptor will smooth, buff and polish – all processes adding demonstrable value – until the final piece is completed. Each step can be shown within the Value Analysis to have added value, what needs to be determined is that the costs associated with each step do not outweigh the value associated with it.

Questions that are raised in Value Analysis are typically: Can this be done cheaper? Can lower cost materials be used? If lower grade materials are used, how is quality affected, does the quantity of scrap (and thus cost) increase? Is the cost and grade of the labour optimum? Can the speed of the process be improved? Should we buy or make components?

Positive Views on Model	Negative Views on Model
• Structured, systematic approach to assessing value and cost • Commonly used model to challenge processes	• Value Analysis, Value Engineering and Value Mapping are often confused • Time-consuming process

Ethical & Environmental

22. 8R Model of Responsible Waste Treatment
23. 4D Model
24. Green Diversity Model
25. Inequality – Types and Principles
26. Nine Dimensions of Sustainability
27. Ohno Seven Wastes
28. 3E Model
29. 3i Model

22. 8R Model of Responsible Waste Treatment

The 8R Model is a sustainability model which highlights the eight main ways product or materials can be managed to extend life, or reduce waste; the most commonly cited "R's" are Reduce, Reuse and Recycle.

The 8R Model highlights eight possible ways to manage waste product reaching the end of its operational life. The traditional model of Reduce, Reuse and Recycle has been adapted with an aim to help highlight alternative options for items to extend their useful life. Whilst in many cases an item may be considered waste to one individual, it may still be serviceable to another. In some cases selling or donating through concepts such as Ebay or Freecycle can help relocate to a new user and thereby extending the life of the product. Equally, remarketing it (using words such as retro, vintage or antique), or remanufacturing it to extend its life (such as remoulding tyres) is important and of use.

8R's	Description	Example
Reuse	Reuse item in its intended role	Second hand items, e.g. clothes, cars, equipment
Resell	Resell item for use by another	Ebay and other classified ad sales channels
Removal	Remove from the market for storage	Old fire-engines are often retained in a remote storage location for retrieval in the event of a major incident
Remarket	Remarket the item in a new light	At a certain age an old car becomes a "vintage car", similarly furniture becoming an antique
Return to Manufacturer	Return the item for dismantling and raw material recovery	Stock cleanse items, old equipment, project surplus materials
Reclaim	Extraction of components for use in other repairs or production	BAE Systems Reduce to Produce programme of taking serviceable parts out of old aircraft for continued use
Remanufacture	Re-manufacture to extend the life of the raw materials	Car maintenance programmes, re-treading of tyres, refilling of gas cylinders
Recycle	Recover raw materials from an end of life asset	Scrap metal dealers, rare earth metal recovery from electronic items

Positive Views on Model	Negative Views on Model
• Useful *aide memoire* • Drives initiatives	• No direct guidance • There are other solutions not included in the 8R list

Ethical & Environmental

23. 4D Model

The 4D model helps and individual identify a Conflict Of Interest (COI) and provides guidance as the key steps that need to occur to manage the situation in line with ethical best practice.

A Conflict Of Interest occurs when a person's involvement within an organisation is compromised by their personal aspirations and includes multiple interests that could influence their decisions in favour of their own gain; to identify if there is a potential COI the buyer may ask 4 questions:

- Will I gain financially in addition to my salary?
- Do I have any personal relationships with colleagues or suppliers?
- Am I doing an identical role for a competitor?
- Should I disclose any of my concerns?

If the answer to any of the first three questions is "yes" they should disclose their interest so it can be addressed to ensure no unethical behaviour occurs and that the organisation's code of ethics is not breached. The 4D model outlines how to deal with conflicts of interest:

Action	Explanation
Disclose	**Disclose** the potential conflict of interest to the organisation.
Distance	If having disclosed the potential COI, the individual should not have direct input with the contract and should **distance** themselves from the associated deal.
Delegate	If the person is unable to distance themselves from working on the deal, they should **delegate** the task to a colleague who has no COIs with the supplier.
Disassociate	When a COI occurs within an organisation's critical contracts, the procurement professional could **disassociate** themselves from the deal to ensure complete objectivity in the contract process.

Positive Views on Model	Negative Views on Model
• Provides a structured and systematic process for escalating a solution to COI's	• Model does not disclose how to police such behaviours

24. Green Diversity Model

Diversity in the workplace relates to the differences between individuals focusing on race, gender, ethnicity, age, religion, sexual orientation and disability which research has shown generates an improvement in operational performance, generation of innovation and improved moral.

The Green Diversity Model (2018) – highlighted several practices that increase the value and respect for diversity in the workplace:

Practice	Explanation
Diversity training	In order that staff have the right skills and an increased awareness of diversity.
Financial assistance	Support from the government in terms of grants and reasonable adjustments to allow those with disabilities to have their unique needs
Specific initiatives	Introducing specific initiatives for particular groups, such as support for women returning to the workplace after maternity leave or a period of caregiving provided to minority groups.
Support for the physically disabled	Schemes promoting employment amongst physically disabled people such as vocational counselling and guidance, self-advocacy, the provision of adapted transport and flexible work schedules
Developing an inclusive climate	Developing and maintaining a culture of inclusion with structural support for diverse groups will help specific initiatives to achieve.

Differences should be cultivated to encourage creative ideas and perspectives with compelling research showing a strong correlation between diversity and improved performance.

Positive Views on Model	Negative Views on Model
• Helps positive approaches to improving diversity in the workplace • Aligns with some international legislation such as the Equalities Act 2010	• Some diversity areas are omitted • Requires more detail on the type of training required and the skills necessary to promote diversity

Ethical & Environmental

25. Inequality – Types and Principles

The awareness of inequality has raised a raft of legislative constructs and measures intended to ensure that all persons within society are treated equally and fairly within all commercial and day-to-day civilian activities.

The concept of inequality is now high on the agenda in a significant number of countries, embedded in many legal systems and entrenched in the fabric of Procurement, Supply Chain, Management and Ethical best practice. Whether in terms of employment, management or selection of suppliers, an awareness pf the need to ensure equality in society and in commercial best practice is not a new one. During the 1970s across the world, society started to look at introducing equality measures on a number of different aspects including race, gender, religion, age, disability and more latterly sexuality.

With the global move towards this equitable mandate, old legislation – such as the UK Settlement Act 1701 which prevented UK Catholics from equal rights to Anglican members of the population – was repealed and a series of legislative efforts were introduced in many legal domains including the WTO, EU, EU, UK and others. There are four specific EU Directives and the UK Equality Act 2010 introduced to ensure compliance.

To remember the different areas of discrimination the acronym DROP GAMES is a useful aide memoire:

Disability	Gender
Religion	Age
Orientation	Marital Status
Pregnancy	Ethnicity
	Sexual Orientation

Increasingly, the punishment for breaches of equality are becoming more severe with fines and even prison sentences levied in some legal domains.

Positive Views on Model	Negative Views on Model
• Provides a useful aide memoire as an exam reminder	• Merely a list, no demonstrable output

26. Nine Dimensions of Sustainability

The Nine Dimensions model expands the Triple Bottom Line or Three Pillar model to add definition to each Pillar: the People Pillar considers Character, Company and Community (C); the Profit Pillar looks at Sales, Service and Strategy (S); and the Planet Pillar adopts Reduce, Reuse and Recycle (R).

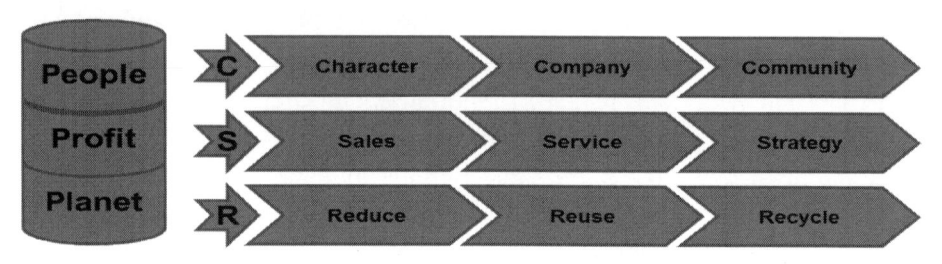

People	C	Character	Company	Community
Profit	S	Sales	Service	Strategy
Planet	R	Reduce	Reuse	Recycle

The Triple Bottom Line model is an established model which suggests sustainability can be considered using three pillars labelled – Social, Economic and Environmental, or People, Profit and Planet, and subsequently has been expanded to help illustrate the core elements which make a strong pillar, and help students expand exam answers. The People Pillar needs to consider the needs of the person or Character, its own Company requirements and the needs of the wider Community to ensure a long-term supply of future employees and suppliers.

Equally there are three dimensions which are required to make a sustainable profit – a strong Sales structure, a good Service delivery to maintain the customers, and a Strategy to ensure that the profit is maintained over the period – and three considerations to ensure best use of natural resources – Reducing what is used, Reusing where possible and Recycling product and/or raw materials. Finally, the third column in the model references the need to future proof strategy, i.e. think about your personnel needs in the future through effective nurturing of new talent, think about new customer needs and recover raw materials to prevent scarcity issues curtailing future deliveries.

Positive Views on Model	Negative Views on Model
• Highlights how the *Pillars* and thus a CSR policy can be developed and made effective	• No indication of what should be in each dimension or how the CSR process and policy should be constructed

Ethical & Environmental

27. Ohno Seven Wastes

The Ohno Seven Wastes are considered the seven aspects of waste that an organisation generates in its operational activity. Ohno showed that analysing and removing these wastes would improve the efficiency, effectiveness and competitiveness of the organisation.

Originating from within the Toyota organisation and the Toyota Production System (TPS), Ohno identified seven wastes that needed to be eliminated to improve the operational excellence of the organisation. These are at the centre of the Toyota ethos on elimination of waste within their production and operation processes. The seven wastes are listed below and can be remembered by the TIMWOOD acronym:

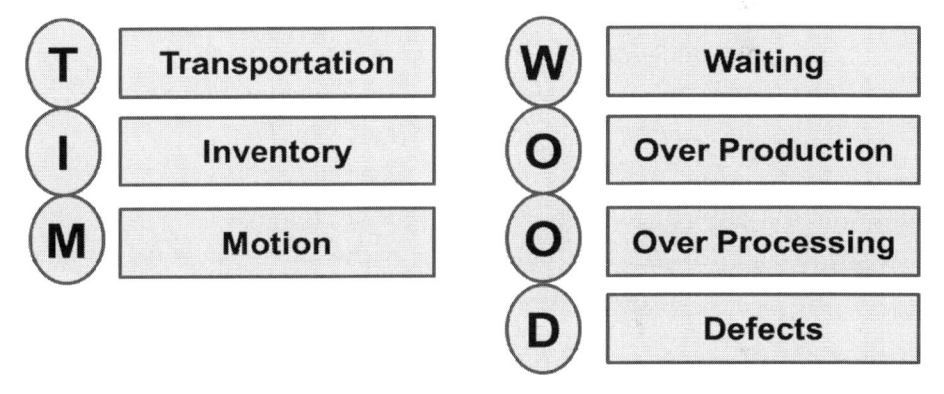

T	Transportation	W	Waiting
I	Inventory	O	Over Production
M	Motion	O	Over Processing
		D	Defects

Since the publication of the Ohno Seven Wastes, there has in fact been an eighth waste added – production of an output which does not meet the customer expectations, or is not used as initially intended, or is not using all the potential of the human resource in the business.

When engaging in cost reduction activities, analysis and evaluation of each step in the operational process with these wastes in mind helps steer practitioners towards successful identification and elimination of waste.

Positive Views on Model	Negative Views on Model
• Established model highlighting possible location of waste in an organisation's delivery activities • Proven and widely utilised	• Other wastes added afterwards e.g. making something the customer rejects • Other wastes like CO_2 not included.

28. 3E Model

The 3E Model is used to pinpoint and evaluate cost reduction opportunities. These prospective cost reduction ideas will fall generally into one of three areas – Economic, Efficiency, and Effectiveness.

The three different ways of reducing cost in a project generally fall into one of three categories:

- Economic – Obtain a lower cost for the product or service;
- Efficiency – Get more return from the product or service;
- Effectiveness – Use the product or service in a more strategic way.

This is perhaps best explained with an example:

In order to reduce the costs of lighting in a building we could:

1. Lower the price of a unit of electricity (Economy)
2. Make the light sources emit more light for the same power (Efficiency)
3. Use the lighting only when required or in core locations (Effectiveness)

Economy	Efficiency	Effectiveness
• The cost of procuring and using the goods or services	• The comparison between what is and what could have been	• The extent to which the objectives are achieved
• In the lighting example, the cost of the electrical power to run the lighting system	• In the lighting example, choice of light sources will affect the quantity of the light emitted per KWh of power	• In the lighting example, this might include the strategic timing or placement of light fittings

Positive Views on Model	Negative Views on Model
• Easy and simple to remember model useful to identify issues opportunities	• Doesn't focus on structural cost, CAPEX reduction or consequential costs

Ethical & Environmental

29. 3i Model

The 3i Model highlights the different levels of culpability of non-compliance or misrepresentation in a contract or legal circumstance and to some extent drives the determination of remedial action or compensation.

The 3i Model is used in commercial assessments to evaluate the nature and level of input by a defendant in a punitive situation.

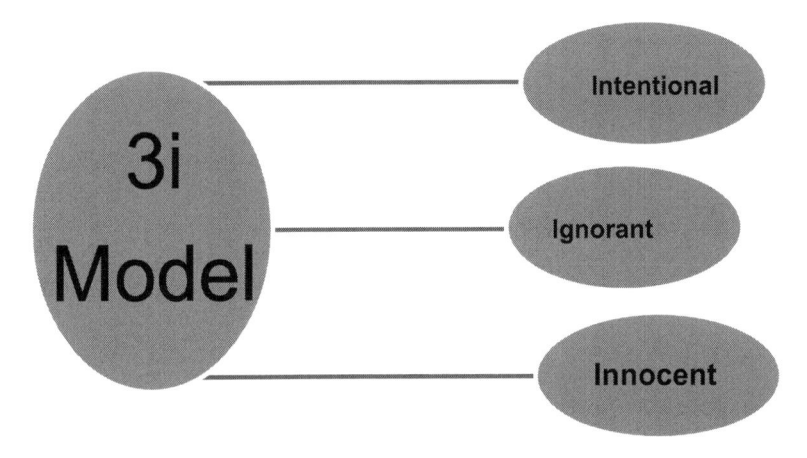

3i Model
- Intentional
- Ignorant
- Innocent

When determining the compensation, penalties or actions that relate to a situation, it is important to consider the sentiments that led to the defendant's actions. Clearly if the actions were premeditated (Intentional) then the legal approach will be more severe than if the defendant is unaware of the impact of his or her actions.

In contrast where the defendant is unaware, a more lenient approach will often be taken. However, this lack of awareness stems from two situations: firstly, should the defendant have known, were they Ignorant; or secondly, how reasonable is it to suggest that the defendant should have known, were they Innocent in their actions.

Positive Views on Model	Negative Views on Model
• Gives clarity in commercial disputes	• Giving a determination on ignorance vs innocence is often very difficult and subjective

Human Resource Management

30. Belbin Team Roles
31. Crocker Triangle
32. Eysenck Hierarchical Model of Personality
33. Goleman's domains of emotional intelligence
34. Hofstede Cultural Factors Model
35. Honey & Munford learning styles
36. HR RITUAL
37. Johnson Cultural Web
38. RACI Assessment
39. Rodgers Seven Point Plan
40. Training Needs Analysis Vanguard Model

30. Belbin Team Roles

Belbin identified and examined the different roles that people take within an a team or organisation. Belbin categorised these into Action, Social and Thinking roles with individuals having a tendency to trend towards one main role.

Belbin recognised that when formulating a team it is critical to ensure that there is a blend of roles within the team, and that each individual had a tendency towards a certain role behaviour. Having all of one type of role type in a team will lead to an unbalanced team and often result in skewed results and outcomes, such instances in history include the "Bay of Pigs" incident in Cuba and arguably the "Second Iraq War".

Action
- Completer Finisher - Focuses on what is required to complete the project
- Implementer - Drives the implementation of ideas within the team
- Shaper - Steers direction and scope of the project or team activity

Social
- Co-ordinator – Co-ordinates people and resources within the team
- Resource Instigator - Ensures all resources are obtained as required
- Team Worker - Supports team activity, willing to undertake tasks

Thinking
- Monitor Evaluator - Manages milestones, objectives and measurement
- Specialist - Team player who has specialist skills or technical input
- Plant – Generates ideas and direction of the project

In a project setting, if the team is full of specialists, for example, there is a chance that the project will not be finished or will be delivered late. If a team is full of monitor evaluators, then the team will be worried about progress and quality and less focused on idea generation or deadlines.

Positive Views on Model	Negative Views on Model
• Identifies core instinct of people • Improves balance of teams	• Rarely used as a starting point when developing teams • Individual may mask core nature for personal reasons

31. Crocker Triangle

The Crocker Triangle examines the enormous savings and operational opportiunities that can be made by Procurement facilitating the use of internal and external Cross-Functional Teams (CFTs).

The Crocker Triangle highlights the inter-relationships between client internal operations, the client's user interface and the service provider, and highlights the activity required to add value in each of the three direct interactions shown on the three arrows.

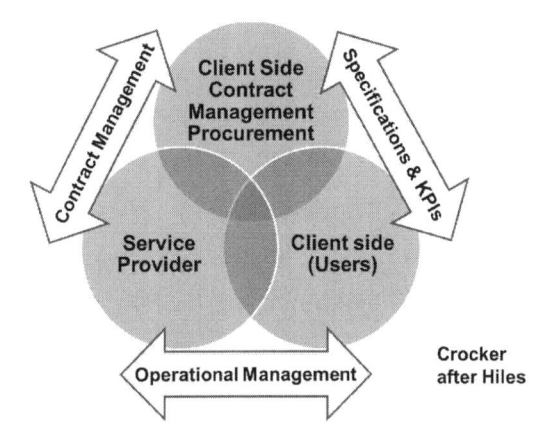

Crocker after Hiles

Internally, close co-operation between Procurement, Production, Finance and R&D, alongside external interactions with Suppliers, can result in benefits in three key areas:

- Leverage buying power (Renegotiating contracts and re-bundling volumes)
- Leverage product improvements (standardisation, design to cost and value analysis)
- Optimise processes (reduce joint costs and waste reduction)

Advantages of CFTs are continuous improvements and lower TCO, though there are often difficulties of information flows and synchronisation.

Positive Views on Model	Negative Views on Model
• Aligns internal relationships with team activity • Highlights operational activity needed to add the value	• Other areas such as risk need to be addressed using other models in parallel

32. Eysenck Hierarchical Model of Personality

The Eysenck Hierarchical Personality Model assesses personality against two core dimensions – neuro-stability and extraversion – characterising people into one of four corresponding segments: Melancholic, Choleric, Phlegmatic and Sanguine.

The Eysenck Model utilises two diverse dimensions of personality – neuro-stability and extraversion to analyse participants in a question orientated evaluation. The outcomes from the review would in theory position the person into one segment in a four-segment model with each segment labelled as follows: Melancholic, Choleric, Phlegmatic and Sanguine.

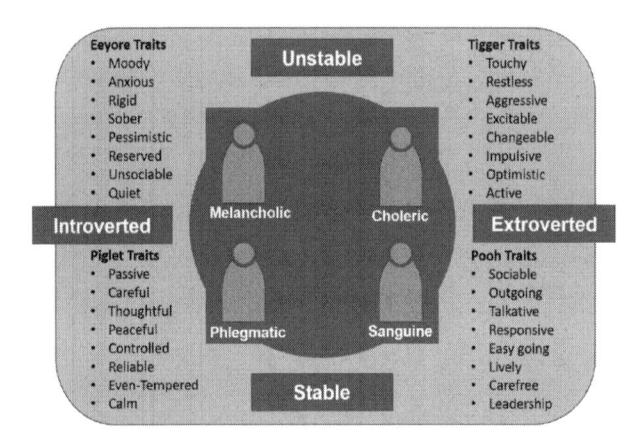

Whilst not part of the original construct, by coincidence these four segments relate very closely with A.A.Milne's Winnie the Pooh characters – Tigger representing Choleric, Eeyore Melancholic, Piglet Phlegmatic, and Pooh Sanguine.

The Eysenck Personality Questionnaire (EPQ) is used to assess the employees based on their emotional stability and thus the predictability of their personality orientated responses in certain situations, coupled with their levels of introvert or extrovert behaviours ensuring the right types of people are involved in project teams, especially in complex situations. It is often used with other OPQs such as Myers Briggs and DISC.

Positive Views on Model	Negative Views on Model
• Utilises two clear and different dimensions to assess and evaluate employee personality	• This is one of a number of personality appraisal options which sometimes produce conflicting output.

33. Goleman's Domains of Emotional Intelligence

Goleman defines Emotional Intelligence - often abbreviated to EI - as "the capacity for recognising our own feelings and those of others, for motivating ourselves, and for managing emotions well in ourselves as well as others".

Goleman's Emotional Intelligence Model has five basic components of Emotional Intelligence which are explained below; Higgs and Reynolds (2002) adapted the domains for procurement and Supply Chain functions:

Self Awareness	Knowing what we are feeling in the moment and using those preferences to guide our decision making whilst cognisant of personal ability and self-confidence
Self Regulation	Handling our emotions so that they facilitate rather than interfere with the task at hand; being conscientious and delaying gratification to pursue goals
Motivation	Using our deepest preferences to move and guide us towards our goals, to help us take initiative and strive to improve and persevere in the face of setbacks and frustrations
Empathy	Sensing what people are feeling, being able to take their perspective, and cultivating rapport and atonement with a broad diversity of people
Social Skills	Handling emotions in relationships, reading social situations; interacting smoothly; using skills to persuade and lead, negotiate, settle disputes and for cooperative teamworking

Positive Views on Model	Negative Views on Model
• Useful skills for leaders	• No direct guidance
• Helps to use our other skills	• Needs to explain feedback

34. Hofstede Cultural Factors Model

Hofstede identified five core characteristics of national identity: Power Distance; Long Term Perspective; Uncertainty Avoidance; Masculinity; and Individualism. Each nation he examined displayed tendencies towards different combinations of these traits and exhibited different weightings.

Understanding the typical people traits of a nation helps explain: the reaction to a suggestion such as a commercial pitch; the response you may receive from a new idea; the urgency with which a decision is made; the different reactions to male and female pressures; the power hierarchy; decision processes; and the time to get agreements. These can be seen at the website www.hofstede.com. For example:

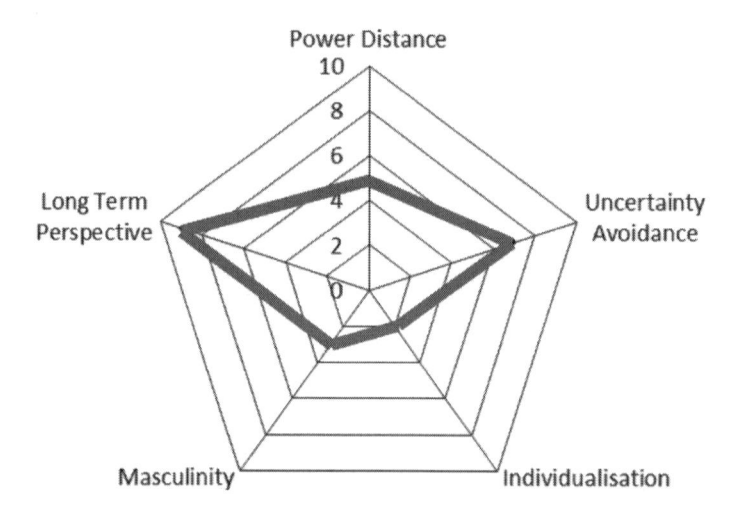

Take different nations with which you are familiar and compare them to the Hofstede model. Be careful with larger nations where there may be diverse characteristics, for example in Nigeria there are large tribal trends that differ from North to South which may skew any findings, or the United States where different states may have differing behaviours, for example compare Alaska with Arizona, Wyoming and West Virginia.

Positive Views on Model	Negative Views on Model
• Identifies characteristics with which many people can associate	• The model aggregates personality characteristics.
• Simple to identify general traits of a nation and avoid issues	• Model only looks at extreme characteristics

35. Honey & Mumford Learning Styles

Honey & Mumford drew up a popular classification of learning styles with individuals having a natural preference to one style. Their research identifyied that people vary not just in learning skills but also in styles.

The Honey and Mumford research identified four key learning styles that individuals favour as follows:

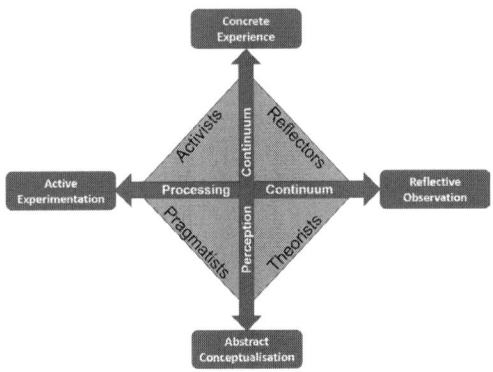

- Theorists need to understand underlying concepts prior to any hands-on attemp – their preferred approach is intellectual and rational;
- Reflectors need to stand back and observe and think deeply about things, considering all angles and analysing all available data, before acting or coming to carefully though-out conclusions;
- Activists need to work on practical tasks or problems and want to "get stuck in".
- Pragmatists need to see a direct link between the subject being studied and a real-world task or problem for which they are or may be responsible; they see no purpose in learning for its own sake.

Awareness of learning styles allows managers/leaders to devise learning activities which are more appropriate to fit the stakeholder's preferences, and therefore work to their strengths. This avoids the frustration of stakeholders being exposed to learning experiences in a form which would be unhelpful and unproductive.

Positive Views on Model	Negative Views on Model
• Engages participants • Drives training effectiveness	• No style is better than another • Other styles may indeed stretch

36. HR RITUAL

The HR RITUAL is an acronym model which looks at the HR cycle from recruitment to leaving. It helps highlight the importance of each element through the lifecycle of an employee – from Recruitment through Induction, Training, Utilisation, Appraisal and concluding with the Leaving – and drive initiatives to develop better induction or appraisal processes.

The HR RITUAL assesses each phase of the employment cycle to highlight the importance of each component to the successful maintenance of an engaged and effective workforce.

The cycle commences with the recruitment of the employee, with attention to aspects such as the job advertisement, the publication media and pre-interview correspondence. This is followed with the Interview process which needs to assess the individual against structured criteria, (See model 39 Rodgers 7 Point Plan). The employee is then trained, utilised and appraised (hopefully at least annually) throughout his career before final departure either to a new job or retirement.

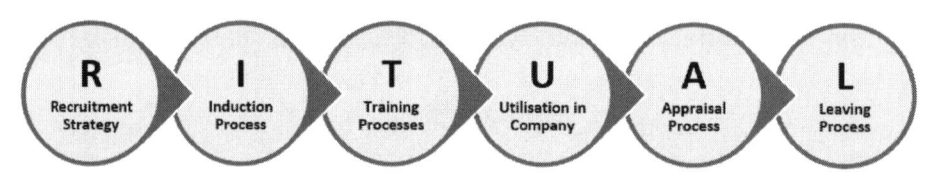

R	I	T	U	A	L
Recruitment Strategy	Induction Process	Training Processes	Utilisation in Company	Appraisal Process	Leaving Process

Following the cessation of activities, a leaver interview should be undertaken as valuable information can be obtained from people leaving an organisation. These may include a plethora of different aspects including dissatisfaction, salary or pay trends in the market, internal issues such as bullying or substandard personnel management, or merely a lack of interest or boredom.

Positive Views on Model	Negative Views on Model
• Gives a clear end to end HR process to ensure best practice • Helps reduce staff turnover and improve morale	• Needs independent process for each element • No feedback loops included

37. Johnson Cultural Web

The Johnson "Cultural Web" (1987) identifies the aspects that drive the formation of the culture in an organisation, these include: Stories/Myths, Symbols, Power and Organisational Structure, Systems and Rituals.

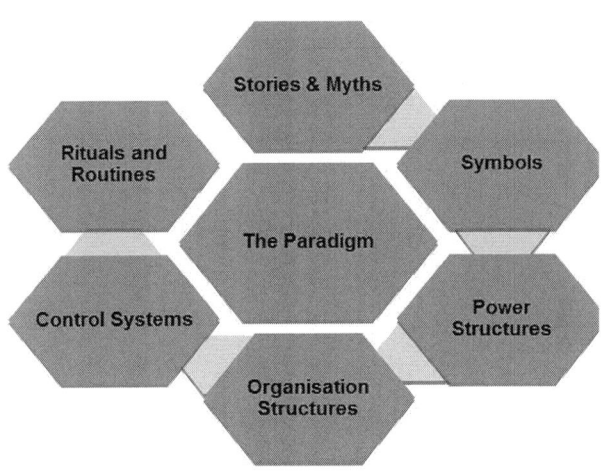

The Cultural Web incorporates six aspects referred to as "Cultural Paradigms", considered as aspects that generate culture in an organisation. These drivers of corporate culture are further split into Soft Drivers (Rituals & Routines, Stories & Myths, and Symbols) which are hard and time consuming to manage, and Hard Drivers (Organisation Structures, Control Systems and Power Structures) which can be planned and introduced in a more planned and direct manner.

Understanding how the culture develops helps management steer or blend the culture by proactively or reactively changing the structures and processes in the organisation. These may include changes to training, work-groups, recruitment, marketing or operating structure, processes. More difficult to address is the eradication of negative history, stories, legends and engrained rituals that have evolved over time.

Positive Views on Model	Negative Views on Model
• Identifies the core elements which management can influence • Allows recognition of past in cultural development	• Culture difficult to define • More than one culture can co-exist in an organisation • Low consideration of external effects such as economy or society

38. RACI Assessment

The RACI (Responsible, Accountable, Consulted and Informed) philosophy focuses on clarifying what stakeholders' roles are and their responsibilities in the context of the specific task or process step.

The main application of the RACI matrix may be used to:
- Specify the involvement of various stakeholders in a project;
- Supplement the Stakeholder power/interest analysis.

The approach works best when the following are adopted:
- There is only one Accountable person to avoid confusion;
- Limited Responsible persons involved to one to avoid duplication;
- A Responsible and an Accountable person must be assigned to every level of activity;
- Confirms the roles and activities assigned with all stakeholders.

**Responsible
Accountable
Consulted
Informed**

The different Stakeholders assume roles within a project ranging from being directly responsible through to merely being informed about the outcomes.

Positive Views on Model	Negative Views on Model
• Gives stakeholders clarity about roles and responsibilities • Ensures each activity has all the RACI roles assigned • Highlights inconsistencies and duplications over authority	• Does not assign relationships between stakeholders • Accountability often over used as ideally a single person should be accountable in a project or contract

39. Rodgers Seven Point Plan

The Rodgers Seven Point Plan identifies seven core areas that need to be explored in the recruitment process, such as intelligence, background, skills, attainment, attitude, physical ability and life interests.

The Rodgers Seven Point Plan recognises the core elements that need to be assessed in a recruitment process, to ensure that the individual selected meets the needs of the business at an operational, intellectual, physical and motivational level. The model considers the following seven points that need consideration:

- Intelligence - The intelligence of the person
- Background - The person's background
- Attainment - Their attainment
- Aptitude - Special aptitudes or skills
- Interests - The candidate's personal interests
- Physical - The person's physical condition
- Disposition - The person's disposition

Ideally all of these areas should be explored through effective questioning or assessments in the interview process to establish whether the person is fit for purpose both in the short, medium and over the longer term.

Furthermore, the job role or specification is an integral part of the process and will need to be considered in how this is achieved as some roles will be more likely to evolve over time. In such circumstances, higher levels of intelligence and the right disposition would be required and the individual may require a background that is more accommodating to development, learning and change.

Positive Views on Model	Negative Views on Model
<ul><li>Provides a clear statement of core areas that need assessing in the interview process.</li><li>Gives guidance when determining interview strategy</li></ul>	<ul><li>No tie-in to other models such as Belbin or other team accredited models.</li></ul>

40. Training Needs Analysis – Vanguard Model

Training Needs Analysis is a systematic approach to ensure capability gaps in an organisation are identified in a time bound way. Training needs must be analysed from the perspective of providing stability to the entire organisational system including demands from the external and internal environment.

Seddon and Brand's (2008) Vanguard Model is a structured approach to the analysis of the skills that personnel need in an organisation to fulfil its corporate and strategic objectives. The process is commonly referred to as Training Needs Analysis and must tie-in with the procurement function's future strategy and plan. The Vanguard Model offers three stages to review training needs analysis:

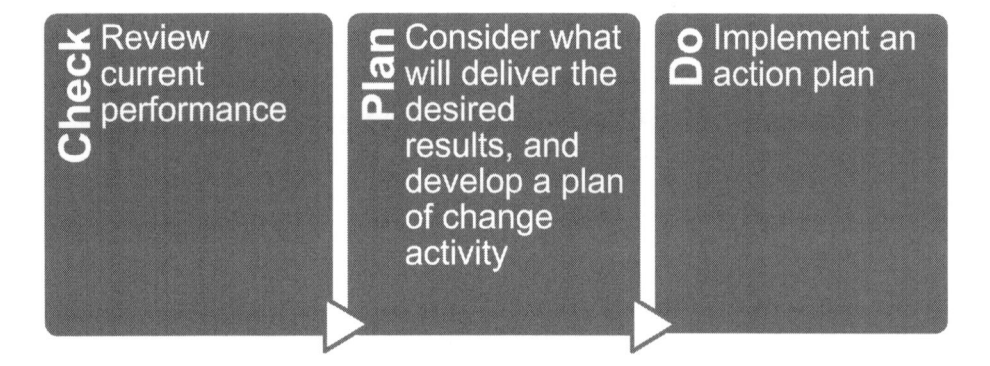

Check	Plan	Do
Review current performance	Consider what will deliver the desired results, and develop a plan of change activity	Implement an action plan

The aim is to have a map of organisational needs both for the prevailing activities as well as to meet future strategic objectives and in some cases projected risks. The primary focus is on improving the value of the human capital within the organisation.

Positive Views on Model	Negative Views on Model
• Helps to identify potential developmental solutions • Maps organisational needs that focus on improving the value of human capital	• Care must be taken to avoid "analysis paralysis" • There are other solutions not included in the 8R list

Management & Leadership

41. Adair Action-Centred Leadership Model
42. Ashridge Management Styles
43. Cialdini Six Principles of Persuasion
44. Fayol Principles of Management
45. Greiner Growth Model
46. Hersey-Blanchard Model
47. Herzberg Hygiene/Motivators
48. Hierarchy of Objectives
49. Maslow Hierarchy of Needs
50. McKinsey 7S Model
51. Mintzberg 5P Model
52. Mintzberg Management Roles
53. Mullins Process of Management Model
54. Nadler and Tushman Congruence Model
55. Organisational Balance Model
56. Senge Five Disciplines
57. Theory X, Theory Y and Theory Z
58. Trait Theory
59. Trist and Bamforth Socio-Technical Approach
60. Tuckman Team Development including Jenson & Robbins

41. Adair Action-Centred Leadership Model

Adair identified three specific characteristics that are important when looking at the management of an organisation: The Task, The Group dynamics and the Individuals therein. The model suggests that leadership can be learned, and people are not necessarily born leaders.

Adair's research was based at Sandhurst Military Training Academy in 1979 and focused on the leadership of a group concluded that there are three specific facets which hold importance – Task, Group and Individuals – and that leadership can be taught and is not determined at birth.

The overlap areas between the three characteristics are important areas of development and where management focus can effect change and create dynamic value.

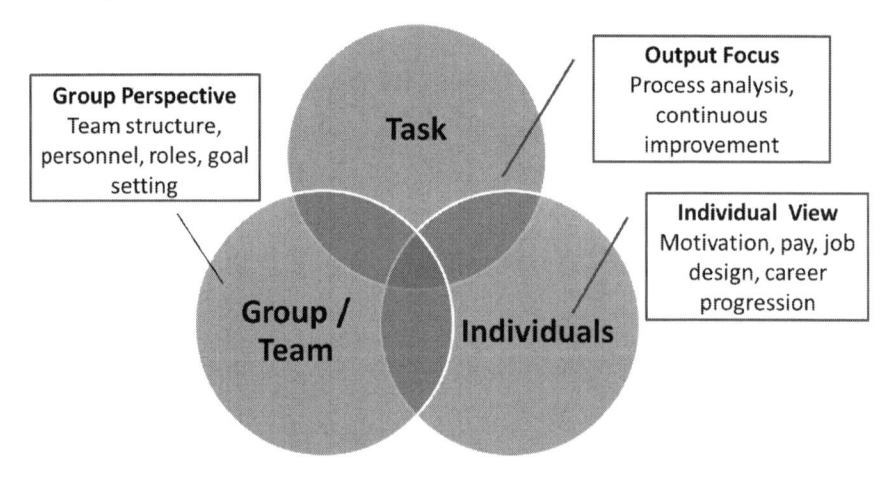

Group Perspective
Team structure, personnel, roles, goal setting

Task

Output Focus
Process analysis, continuous improvement

Group / Team

Individuals

Individual View
Motivation, pay, job design, career progression

For example, team bonding is clearly a major part of the Group or Team element, however improving this will help enhance the contribution and commitment of the individual. Equally, the delivery of output on time, quality and budget will be greatly enhanced if there is a team commitment.

Positive Views on Model	Negative Views on Model
• Highlights the core elements of a great leader • Helps focus on core aspects	• Works best in an autocratic environment • Some view this as outdated and over simplistic

Management & Leadership

42. Ashridge Management Styles

The Ashridge Management Styles focus on how a leader delivers a message to a team and identifies four classic types of message conveyance: Tells, Sells, Consults and Joins.

The Ashridge model identifies four core styles of transmitting message from management to the employees. Each style has its time and place and certain organisations, industries or operations may have a tendency towards one particular style.

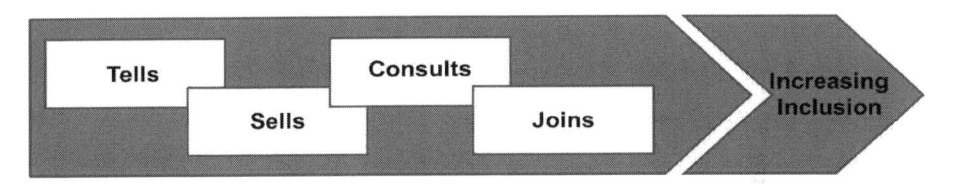

[Diagram: Tells → Sells → Consults → Joins, with arrow indicating "Increasing Inclusion"]

Tells – The leader tells the team players what needs to occur. There is no dialogue, orders are given – imagine a General in the army, for example, he or she will most likely adopt a "Tell" solution due to the strict hierarchical structure.

Sells – The leader uses selling skills to highlight the benefits of following the commands. They would have an answer for any objections and negate objectors, they would carefully use open and closed questions and would focus on obtaining a decision.

Consults – The leader would use consultation to obtain ideas and some buy-in. The ideas would then be fashioned into a proposal and then delivered. There would be buy-in as a result of the process as people know that the outcome reflects the team's ideas.

Joins – A far more collaborative process where identified team players discuss options, arrange process, agree direction and implement as a unified body; some Scandinavian organisations adopt a high level of "Joins" to ensure total buy-in to a project solution.

Positive Views on Model	Negative Views on Model
• Highlights four distinct methods of communication and identifies the impact and consequences of each	• Assumes that management-subordinate relationships act the same in every scenario • No reflection of criticality or risk

43. Cialdini Six Principles of Persuasion

The Cialdini Principles of Persuasion identifies six primary aspects that should be focused on to ensure a successful negotiation and persuasion outcome: Reciprocity, Scarcity, Authority, Consistency, Liking and Consensus.

In order to secure the deal, Cialdini showed that giving first generates an urge for the other part to give something back, and generating a feeling that the item or service is a scarce commodity also helps.

Reciprocity
If someone gives you something, you are more likely to be persuaded to give back

Consistency
People commit more if concept is consistent with things they've committed to previously

Scarcity
When a good or service becomes more scarce, there is an increased desire to have it

Liking
Persuasion is easier with people like us, who compliment us and who cooperate with us

Authority
People are more likely to follow the lead of credible and knowledgeable experts

Consensus
People look to The actions of others to validate and determine their own

Furthermore, if the deal is consistent with past behaviour, is backed by an authoritative expert or role model, is offered by someone we like and we can see it has been endorsed by other people we are much more likely to agree and commit.

For each facet the improvements in the commitments are significant but collectively they are potentially huge.

Positive Views on Model	Negative Views on Model
• Model highlights with evidence the key areas to aid persuasion • Succinct in its output	• Just one of several models which highlight similar concepts

44. Fayol Principles of Management

The Fayol Principles of Management identifies the 14 characteristics that are key traits of a successful manager and aspects that they must address.

Fayol identified 14 aspects that are critical for a successful manager to focus on and address, i.e. the things a manager should ensure happen as a norm within their organisational remit.

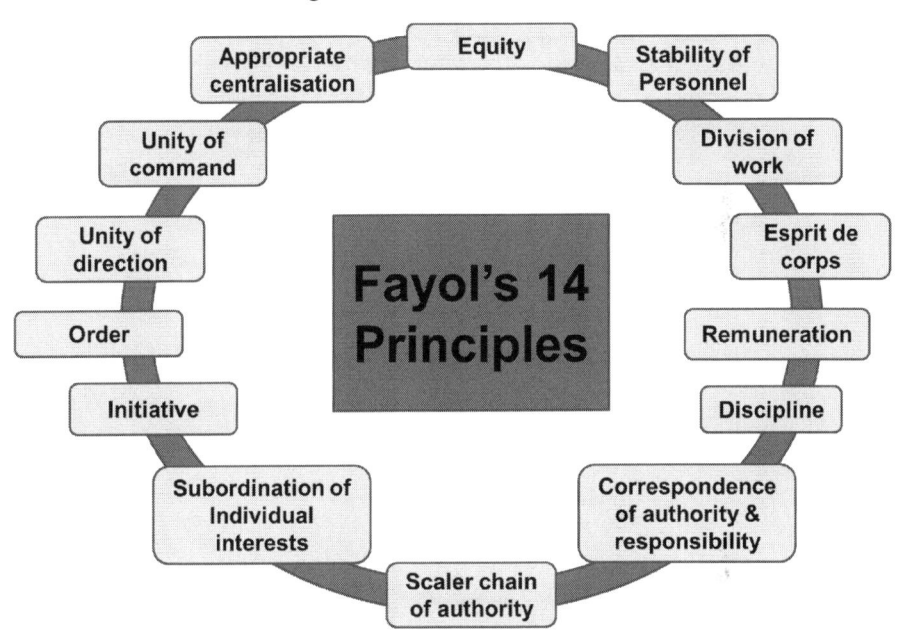

Fayol's 14 Principles:
- Appropriate centralisation
- Equity
- Stability of Personnel
- Division of work
- Esprit de corps
- Remuneration
- Discipline
- Correspondence of authority & responsibility
- Scaler chain of authority
- Subordination of Individual interests
- Initiative
- Order
- Unity of direction
- Unity of command

Clearly aspects such as "discipline", "recognition of the managerial authority" and "personnel issues" are core but "showing initiative" and "generating a clear direction" are activities where the manager has a leadership responsibility and are of equal importance.

Positive Views on Model	Negative Views on Model
• Identifies the core elements of a day to day management role • Good for mechanistic activities with a clear hierarchy of control	• Fails to address strategic activities or vision • Very now focused low future proofing

45. Greiner Growth Model

The Greiner Growth Model identifies six distinct stages within an organisation's expansion and recognises this growth cycle will encounter clear evidence of "crisis" caused by the catalyst driving the evolution.

The Greiner Growth Model identified six areas of growth starting with the early creativity or development of the new idea or business concept. This flows through until there is a leadership crisis when the size of the business demands a review of the management structure.

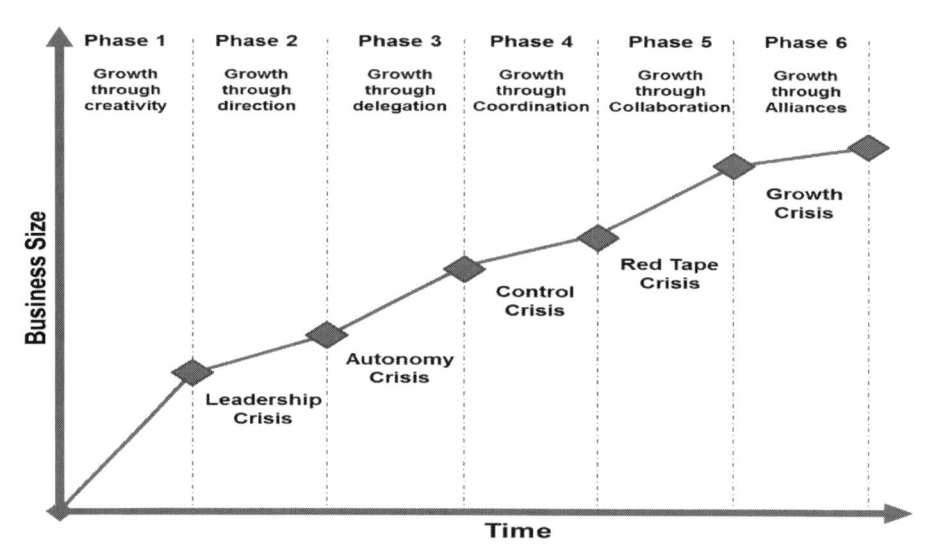

Phase 1	Phase 2	Phase 3	Phase 4	Phase 5	Phase 6
Growth through creativity	Growth through direction	Growth through delegation	Growth through Coordination	Growth through Collaboration	Growth through Alliances

Crises in order: Leadership Crisis, Autonomy Crisis, Control Crisis, Red Tape Crisis, Growth Crisis.

(Axes: Business Size vs Time)

Once appointed, the management team will enable the organisation to grow under their guidance, yet there comes a time when the workers need autonomy to guide themselves; this is the autonomy crisis. Next comes a phase where delegation is adopted to allow workers to be self-directed but this leads to a control crisis due to a lack of centralised control that is remedied by a phase of coordination which prevails until red tape stifles the business. Finally, the red tape is overcome through a period of collaboration which generates issues over the internal growth of the organisation leading to strategic alliances.

Positive Views on Model	Negative Views on Model
• Highlights the problems that occur with business growth • Helps dismantle issues	• Not all organisations grow in the same way or timescales • Doesn't reflect market issues

46. Hersey-Blanchard Model

Hersey Blanchard suggested that "Change Leadership" depends upon (1) the maturity of the participants, (2) the maturity of the staff for the task and (3) upon how ready the Stakeholders are to adopt change.

Hersey Blanchard considered the type of people in a team or organisation, and tried to assess how ready for leadership roles they were. He concluded that the maturity of the people will determine the way that change is delivered or managed. This may result in the type of team leader selected, whether the leader comes from within the organisation or is recruited without any pre-conceived ideas, without any legacy or baggage, or whether the participants respect prior knowledge or history within the incumbent organisation.

Telling M1
Selling M2
Participating M3
Delegating M4

The model suggests the manner in which the team participants are managed, communicated with and led is important. Hersey-Blanchard suggested that in some circumstance – for example military commanders – management will be through "telling" the team players what to do, with little or no room for subordinate input. Equally, there were some circumstances where the participants should be more closely involved – as is typical in co-operatives or many Japanese organisations.

The levels of maturity are labelled M1-M4 with the higher number being those who are more operationally mature, more willing to change.

Positive Views on Model	Negative Views on Model
• Helps management identify the best way to communicate with its workforce • Identifies when engagement with staff will work best	• Doesn't reflect specific nature of the issue in question • Ignores the untapped resource of the employees • Doesn't differentiate between leadership and management

47. Herzberg Hygiene/Motivators

Herzberg identified two characteristics that apply to an individual, Hygiene factors (things expected to be present but dis-satisfy if they are absent) and Motivators (things not expected but generate delight if they occur).

Herzberg recognised two core types of influence in a scenario which he called Hygiene and Motivators - Hygiene are the factors that you expect to be present. They will not delight you, but they will generate dis-satisfaction if they are not there. In contrast there are Motivators – these are items that you do not expect, but which will delight you if they occur and will help generate positive feelings within the team.

Hygiene Factors
- Management
- Salary
- Security
- HES
- Work Conditions

Creates:
- Satisfaction
- Reduced Dis-satisfaction

In a bank you would expect there to be money available (Hygiene Factor) and would be dis-satisfied if there was not.

Motivator Factors
- Recognition
- Interesting Role
- Opportunities
- Responsibility
- Pride

Creates:
- Motivation
- Increased commitment
- Greater satisfaction

Yet it would be a nice surprise if you were offered a cup of coffee whilst queuing (Motivator), but you would not be disappointed if you did not get one

Positive Views on Model	Negative Views on Model
• Long established and recognised model • Clearly identifies aspects which are considered as mandatory and marginal	• Hygiene and motivators could be user specific • Motivators can become hygiene factors over time • Marginal benefit can reduce over time

48. Hierarchy of Objectives

Procurement competence is the "capability to structure the supply base in alignment with the business priorities of the organisation". An effective procurement function needs therefore to coordinate and align procurement plans, policies and actions to the overall strategic business objectives.

The author Philip Boulton proposes that procurement's contribution to business performance depends on the degree to which procurement capabilities fit and support the business strategy. This highlights the importance of procurement strategy as an intermediate element between business strategy and procurement capabilities.

Mission Statement	Purpose, business area, key values
Organisational Goals	Desired future state, where we want to be
Specific Objectives	Specific targets, what we need to do
Strategic Plans	Broad direction, long term 3-5 years
Tactical Plans	Medium term plans, 1-2 years
Operational Plans	Departmental plans, short term 1 year

Procurement effectiveness is the fit between procurement strategic objectives and procurement activities. "Strategic alignment" and procurement effectiveness are now necessary contributors to competitive advantage and business success.

The general and "top" objectives of organisations must cascade down to the more specific objectives of the business units, functions and individuals.

Positive Views on Model	Negative Views on Model
• Gives clear structure to goal and objective setting • Ensures all goals are aligned across the organisation	• Reduces the focus on individual requirements and making targets SMART • Puts organisation needs ahead of the employee need

49. Maslow Hierarchy of Needs

The Maslow Hierarchy of Needs pyramid examines the aspects of life that an individual seeks to gain from a work engagement, starting with basic physical and physiological needs through to aspects that make an individual feel good about themselves, referred to as Self-Actualisation.

The Maslow Hierarchy of Needs pyramid is a long-established model which identifies, categorises and ranks the various aspects that an individual wants to secure from his or her work activity.

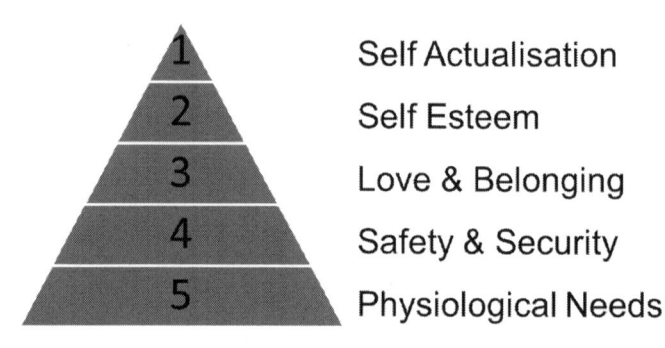

Level	Need
1	Self Actualisation
2	Self Esteem
3	Love & Belonging
4	Safety & Security
5	Physiological Needs

The base of the pyramid are the things that the person looks to sort out in the first instance (Physiological Needs - e.g. food and water), then those in the second tier and so on. The top of the pyramid are the highly desirable aspects that a well-rewarded and thus motivated person may cherish such as experiencing purpose, enjoying a challenge, or the option for creativity.

Notwithstanding this pinnacle, an individual may become despondent if there is nothing left for them to strive for. Good management will ensure that the individual always has something to aim for, a new target, a promotion, extra prestige, or some other motivator.

Positive Views on Model	Negative Views on Model
• Very well established and acknowledged concept • Clearly identifies priorities for an individual	• Different people may have a different pyramid make-up. • The pyramid can change, e.g. upon father or motherhood

50. McKinsey 7S Model

The McKinsey 7S model focuses on a network of seven inter-related core elements that if combined effectively ensures that optimal performance occurs. These elements are divided into tangible, easy to define elements (hard) and others which are less definable (soft) elements.

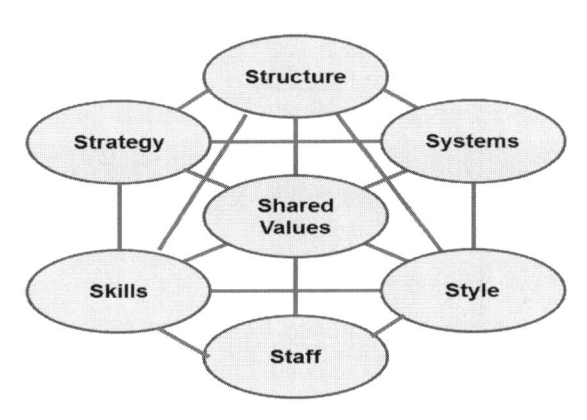

The McKinsey 7S model was created to encourage the production of an effective strategy to examine change, assess delivery resources and enhance performance with a set of common shared values between the parties.

Structure – An organisation with a clear and considered Structure will perform better, be more flexible and will reduce risk;

Systems – Like structure, organised, tried and tested Systems will help improve performance, however compliance is also vital;

Style – The Style of leadership can be important and needs to reflect the nature of the organisation and its stakeholders;

Staff – The quality, motivation and commitment of the Staff and employees or will have a major impact on the organisation's performance;

Skills – Further, the staff need to be well trained and possess the necessary Skills to fulfil their job roles, and unanticipated risks;

Strategy – An organisation will perform better and react to change more quickly if it has a coherent Strategy in place;

Shared Values – And finally, ensuring that the values that exist within the organisation are Shared by the stakeholders.

Positive Views on Model	Negative Views on Model
• A good analysis framework	• No clear outcomes just direction

51. Mintzberg 5P Model

The Mintzberg 5P Model identifies five core areas which need to be considered when developing a business strategy: Planning, Ploys, Patterns, Positioning and Perspective.

Minzberg suggested that there are five core areas around which a strategy is centred. Each is critical to delivery of a specific facet of the strategy and a failure to consider each will undermine its effectiveness:

1. PLAN – An organisation should be aware that strategic PLANning is one core requirement of an effective strategy. This should be a conscious, democratic and structured process;

2. PLOY – We can enhance a strategy by developing PLOYs to out manoeuvre our competitors, in much the same way a General might develop military tactics to outwit an enemy;

3. PATTERN – Further, a strategy could be generated based on our previous PATTERNs of behaviour, i.e. a strategy based on our experience of past activities or performance. A PATTERN may also involve collaboration between several activities to achieve the goal;

4. POSITION – Equally, we need to ensure that we adopt a clear and decisive POSITION in respect of our strategy or a specific point therein;

5. PERSPECTIVE – Finally, we need to understand how the views of others are affected by our strategy by considering their PERSPECTIVE or vision of the future events in the market or organisational life-cycle.

Positive Views on Model	Negative Views on Model
• Helps drive the thought process around the critical aspects which make a strategy successful	• Doesn't necessarily include all factors that are important: e.g. political pressure or previous experience • Doesn't include a review or feedback cycle

52. Mintzberg Management Roles

The Mintzberg Management Rules are a list of ten rules a manager must follow in order to achieve his or her core objectives and ensure managerial success.

Mintzberg identified and categorised 10 key roles that a typical manager needs to possess in order to be effective although not all managers need to comply with all ten roles dependent upon their managerial function. These roles fall into three distinct groupings: Interpersonal, Informational and Decisional.

Category	Mintzberg's Role	Skill Set Required
Interpersonal	**Figurehead** — Employees respect the person's authority	Reputation, assertiveness, confidence, humility and image
Interpersonal	**Leader** — Manager displays leadership skills	Reputation, stature, charisma and emotional intelligence
Interpersonal	**Liaison** — Manager can liaise both internally and externally	Networking, and communication skills
Informational	**Monitor** — Has a good awareness of operating environment	System, industry, market and cultural knowledge
Informational	**Disseminator** — Can effectively communicate with the team	Information management, communication and presentation skills
Informational	**Spokesperson** — Is able to speak-up for the team when required	Negotiation, charisma, communication and presentation skills
Decisional	**Entrepreneur** — Generates ideas, delivers change & solves issues	Vision, initiative, passion and change management skills
Decisional	**Disturbance Handler** — Can help manage, mediate and resolve conflict	Ability to listen, empathy, compassion, focus and fairness
Decisional	**Resource Allocator** — Can manage resources both personnel & funding	Numeric, interpersonal and analytical skills
Decisional	**Negotiator** — Manager is able to negotiate well for the team	Ability to listen, analytical skills, determination and a win-win focus

Positive Views on Model	Negative Views on Model
• Identifies key areas in which a manager needs to perform well • Roles evolve so skills may need to be developed as well	• Roles relate to success of manager not the organisation • Ignores power or ownership as an issue

53. Mullins Process of Management Model

The Mullins Management Model argues that "it is through the process of management that the efforts of the various stakeholders of the organisation are co-ordinated, directed and guided towards the achievement of its goals. Management is the cornerstone of organisational effectiveness".

Mullins suggests that the role of Management is essentially an integrating activity to reconcile and align the needs of people and the needs of the organisation.

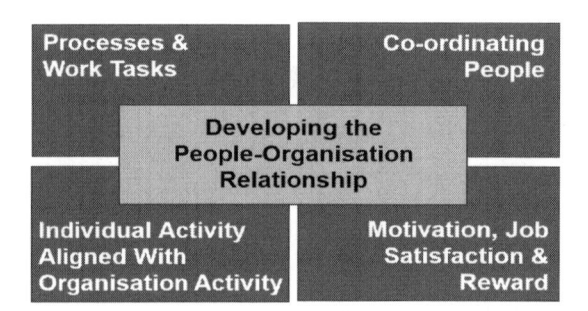

Processes & Work Tasks	Co-ordinating People
Developing the People-Organisation Relationship	
Individual Activity Aligned With Organisation Activity	Motivation, Job Satisfaction & Reward

Management needs to ensure that employees are satisfied and their workspace is positive whilst achieving the strategic goals of the organisation.

The model can be fully explained in more detail as follows:
- Management process is key to delivering organisational performance;
- Managers help to ensure that individual and teamwork tasks align with organisational objectives;
- Human resources present a unique challenge to the process of management as individuals are not alike;
- People processes can be standardised, but the individual's response to them will be unique;
- The manager's role is to create the right conditions for people to deliver the required performance levels and to feel satisfied in their jobs;
- Integrates the operational activity and needs of an organisation with the needs of the individual to maximise effectiveness and efficiency.

Positive Views on Model	Negative Views on Model
• A systematic approach • Uses many key variables of the process	• Fails to recognise that individuals have varying degrees of willingness and readiness for tasks

54. Nadler & Tushman Congruence Model

The Nadler & Tushman Congruence Model examines the operation of the organisation, and its relationship with its employees, structure, culture and work objectives in the context of the environment in which it operates.

Nadler & Tushman identified four forces that were at play in a transformational Process:

- The work tasks that need to be completed;
- The formal systems and structure that exists within the organisation;
- The culture of the organisation;
- How the capabilities of the people within the organisation are used.

The model, is a four-quadrant matrix within an overarching operating structure and forms the basis of organisational responses to demands from the operating environment as depicted below to generate the desirable outcomes both from the corporate and employee perspective:

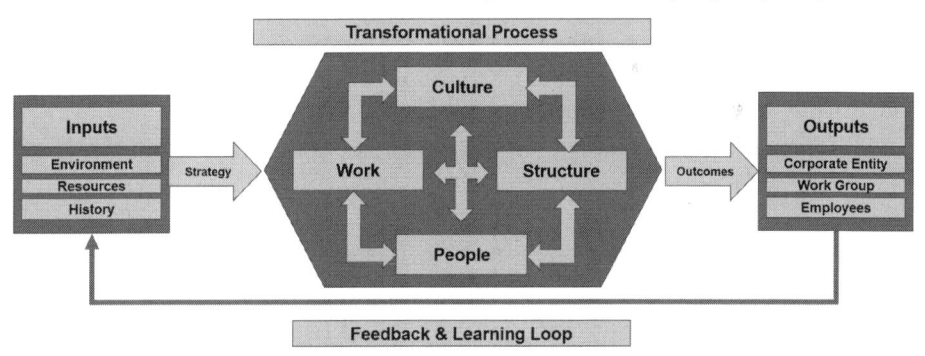

A key observation from this model and process is the identification of employee weaknesses driving training and skills development in the workforce.

Positive Views on Model	Negative Views on Model
• In the short-term congruence is related to effectiveness and performance • Process includes a learning loop to develop best practices	• High congruence can lead to resistance to change • A weakness in any one of the quadrants can increase the resistance to change

55. Organisational Balance Model

Foster's Model of organisational balance (2018) is a people-led approach to organisation design progressing the socio-technical approach of Trist and Bamforth 1951 – Model 59.

The Foster Organisational Balance Model focuses on the interrelationship between human interactions within the organisation and proposes that it is primarily the human system that determines organisation performance. The model aims to increase organisational performance and develop a self-sustaining system by considering the following interrelationships:

Interrelationship	Explanation
The Purpose of the Organisation	The reason why it exists
The Leader in Me – Two Types of Leader	Leaders of people and leaders of expertise.
The Talent Within	Investing resource into identifying, developing and releasing talent.
Harmonious Communities	Using a network of cohesive groups to manage business-related tasks across functions
Organisational Habitat	Developing synergy within the organisation to help the organisation react to and exploit opportunities as they occur.
Organisational Husbandry	A holistic framework where operational decisions are made with awareness of unintended consequences and a commitment to environmental stewardship and citizenship.
Creative Adaptation	Empowering people to innovate and make space for creative problem solving.
Energy Transformation	Use of sustainable practices to ensure change delivers positive impacts with managers accountable for outcomes.
Organisational Cycling	The continuous process of change in response to environmental inputs that move the organisation towards a balance prior to next disruptive force

Positive Views on Model	Negative Views on Model
• Useful *aide memoire* • Very comprehensive	• No direct guidance on skills necessary

Management & Leadership

56. Senge Five Disciplines

The Senge Five Disciplines theory identifies the five core leadership disciplines which are considered useful when implementing change recognising that during such times there is a need to harness all the skills of the workforce and enable them to learn and develop.

The Senge Five Disciplines theory considers the critical need for an organisation to cultivate the learning potential of its workforce during a time of change and maintain their commitment during a time of potentially heightened stress. Recognising this, Senge proposed the five main leadership skills necessary to harness this learning and commitment:

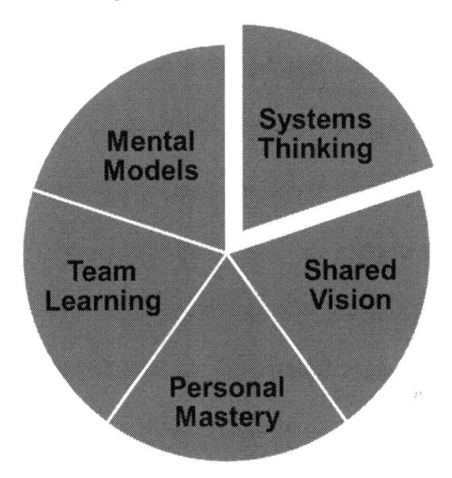

Shared Vision – Helps build commitment and reduces resistance
Personal Mastery – Helps people become self-aware and builds confidence in their own ability

Team Learning – Helps group learning by confronting change in unity

Mental Models – Develops beliefs, values, anxieties and perceptions over the change process

Systems Vision – Increases awareness of the change programme and how it impacts on the organisation, and it unites all the disciplines

Positive Views on Model	Negative Views on Model
• Identifies the leadership focus to effect successful change • Disciplines united by Systems Vision so effort often in tandem	• Learning cultures and environments take time to develop

57. Theory X, Theory Y and Theory Z

Theory X, Y and Z suggest that "people" are one of three core types. Originally McGregor stated that people are either inherently lazy (Type X) or seek work as a motivating activity (Type Y). Ouchi later suggested that there was a third type, people who wanted team involvement and the relationships that this brings.

McGregor's Theory X & Theory Y assumptions suggested that employees in an organisation fell into one of two categories:

1. Employees were either inherently lazy (Theory X) or;
2. Employees actively looked for work as they saw it as a motivating and rewarding endeavour providing stimulus and personal gratification (Theory Y).

Theory X
- People inherently dislike work and are lazy
- People must be coerced or controlled to do work to achieve objectives
- People prefer to be directed
- Motivation is achieved only through pay and basic rewards

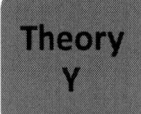

Theory Y
- People view work as being as natural as play and rest, and just as enjoyable
- People will exercise self-direction and self-control towards achieving objectives they are committed to
- People learn to accept and seek responsibility
- Motivation can come from challenges, responsibility and self-esteem needs

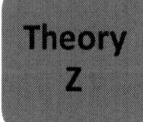

Theory Z
- Aim should be for positive morale of the employee, motivation, and their general happiness
- Strive for stable employment conditions and low staff turnover
- Employer-employee contract leading to loyalty and commitment
- Produces high productivity and contribution levels

Later, Ouchi introduced a third idea entitled "Theory Z" which focused attention on the needs of the team members. These included an individual's desire to be part of a group, to feel they contribute to a team activity and that they derive social benefit from the collective activity.

Positive Views on Model	Negative Views on Model
• Very well established and understood model	• Many consider there to be far more iterations • Model is arguably too simple

58. Trait Theory

Traits are attributes or qualities which create a tendency to behave in a certain manner. Trait Theory assumes that successful managers are born, certain traits are more suitable for certain roles and good managers are good because they have the right combination of personality traits.

Trait Theory suggests that situation and behaviours are at the core of leadership and the traits leaders display.

Stogdill attempted to determine exactly which traits are essential in a leader with his survey of American studies and highlighted the following qualities as being critical:

- Adaptability to situations
- Alertness to social environment
- Dependability
- Self-confidence
- Ambition and achievement orientation
- Willingness to assume responsibility
- Assertive communication
- Tolerance of stress
- Co-operation
- Energy
- Decisiveness
- Persistence
- Dominance

McCall and Lombardo (1983) however took a different perspective and identified the four primary traits required for good leadership:

- Emotional stability and composure
- Admitting errors and weaknesses
- Good interpersonal and communication skills
- Intellectual breadth

Positive Views on Model	Negative Views on Model
• It merely allows people to recognize a leader when they see one • Useful as part of the management selection process	• Does not take into account the individuality of subordinates

59. Trist & Bamforth Socio-Technical Approach

The Socio-Technical Approach to Management of Trist & Bamforth integrated the classical and human relations perspectives by emphasising organisations as complex socio-technical systems, operating as open systems within an external environment.

The Trist & Bamforth Model states that all organisations need both effective technology and coordinating social dynamics in order to be successful. The model advocates an approach called "composite autonomous group working" - composite in terms of the range of skills in a group as a whole (i.e. multi-skilling) and autonomous in terms of self-termination (i.e. in regard to task-organisation and allocation).

The approach acknowledged:

- Although new technology necessitated some change in work organisation, the advantages were counteracted by employee resistance to the loss of psycho-social benefits of working in groups;
- Work organisation is not wholly determined by technology but by organisational choices;
- The existence of subsystems (and their goals) needed to be integrated;
- The organisation must attempt to balance economic, technological and psycho-social needs in its strategic decision-making about work and the employees;
- The need to embrace the dynamic nature of complex organisations;
- There was a clear inter-relationship between the organisation and its external operating environment.

Positive Views on Model	Negative Views on Model
• Focuses on the recognition of people as being crucial in realising overall value • The dynamic nature of an organisation is a key factor	• Based on an analogy that has subsequently been eclipsed by Contingency Theory

60. Tuckman Team Development Cycle

The Tuckman Team Development Cycle(1965) looks at how a team is established and the phases necessary to make the team effective. This model has been added to in recent years however the core content remains the same: FORM-STORM-NORM-PERFORM.

Tuckman suggests that first of all you need to FORM a team, let it have some time to get organised (STORM), let the organisation develop its NORMal practices, and then let the team PERFORM as it is intended.

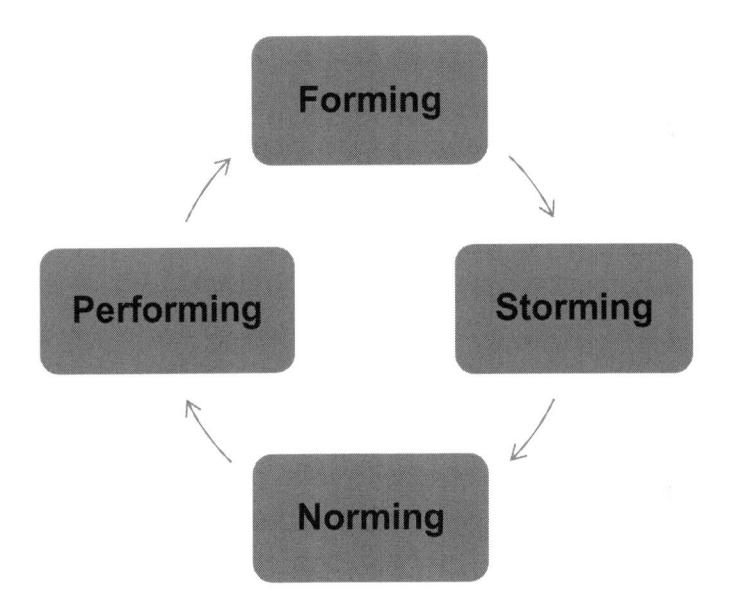

```
         Forming
       ↗        ↘
Performing      Storming
       ↖        ↙
         Norming
```

Later versions of this model including Jenson & Robbins include DORMING, ADJOINING and MOURNING which reflect the fact that after performing you should reflect on the performance and adjust the team before forming again or manage its demise. These are the feedback and adjustment loops within the team development model.

Positive Views on Model	Negative Views on Model
• Helps establish where a team is in its development and what management intervention is needed.	• Only an observational model • Doesn't directly suggest remedy, direction, process or solutions

Market & Price Analysis

61. Ansoff Matrix
62. Boston Consulting Group Matrix & Product Life Cycle
63. Kotler 4P Model
64. Porter Competitive Advantage Model
65. Porter Five Force Model
66. Supply Market Analysis

61. Ansoff Matrix

The Ansoff Matrix is used to identify the best method to adopt when planning to develop the business coverage of an organisation especially with new products or in new markets.

The Ansoff Matrix (1957) is a standard four box matrix used to determine the best strategy for the development of an organisation's product and market strategy. The model identifies four routes to generating business expansion:

Market Development – Uses existing products in new markets.

Market Penetration – Sell more of existing product into existing markets.

Product Development – Introduce new products into existing markets.

Diversification – Market and launch new products into new markets. The four approaches were originally intended to grow the sales volume in the organisation, however the four strategies can equally as well be used to enable the organisation to target higher margin opportunities or customers with a lower risk profile.

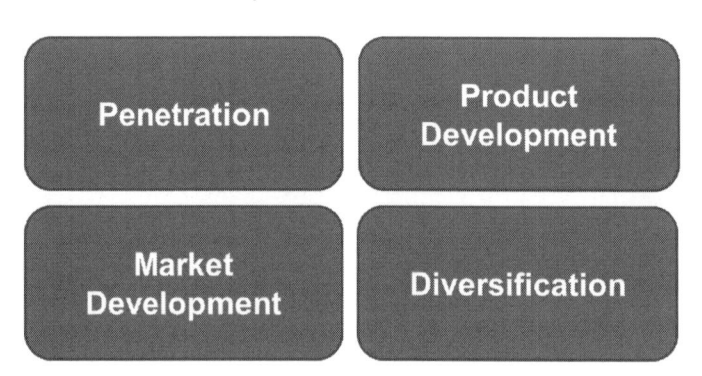

Penetration	Product Development
Market Development	Diversification

Positive Views on Model	Negative Views on Model
• Clearly identifies marketing and product option • Helps plan product diversity and portfolio planning especially if used with Boston Consulting Group Matrix	• Applicable in commercial and FMCG businesses, but limited benefit in Public Sector or charities • Doesn't include the dynamics and nature of the market

62. Boston Consulting Group Matrix & Product Lifecycle

The Boston Consulting Group Matrix is used to identify and categorise products within a corporate product portfolio over the product and market lifecycle. Product categories in this model are: "Question Marks, "Stars", "Cash Cows" and "Dogs".

The Boston Consulting Group Matrix (1984) and corresponding Product Lifecycle are used to categorise products within an organisation's portfolio which are developing or fading.

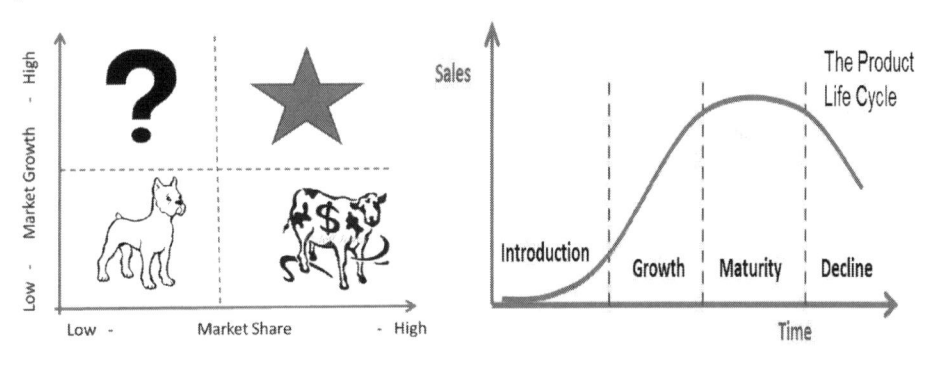

Question Marks are new products in the introductory phase, perhaps from the R&D department; it is uncertain as to whether these will be a success or not. Some will fail others will become Stars and enter the Growth Phase and will become the new flagship products for the company.

Money is spent to launch and publicise these new products, however, in time the product will wane, and marketing funds will cease, as the company seeks to maximise revenue, these are then referred to as Cash Cows in the Maturity Phase. Inevitably over time the Cash Cows will themselves start to wilt and become Dog products and fall into Decline. These may be disposed of or in some cases the product may be re-energised with a marketing regime, it may become fashionable or reach a milestone and be relabelled "retro", vintage or antique.

Positive Views on Model	Negative Views on Model
• Helps identify a proactive product strategy • Helps highlight the need for product innovation and design	• Fails to drive marketing or spend decisions • Only focuses on market share and growth

63. Kotler 4P Model

The Kotler 4P Model is a classic marketing model used at the customer end of the Supply Chain to identify the core ingredients of a correctly marketed product. It should consider the needs and features of the Product, make sure the Price is competitive, in a clear market Place, underpinned with an effective Promotion strategy.

The Kotler 4P Model identifies the four key considerations when marketing a product in a market, and whilst modern Supply Chain philosophy promotes the use of Pull production – i.e. product is only made once a customer has placed a demand – some Supply Chains, particularly in retail, still need to consider the concept of a traditional marketing approach.

The Product needs to be something that the customers in the market want, it must be positioned at a Price that the market can accept or afford, it must be sold in the right Place, and have the right Promotion to allow would-be customers to identify with it.

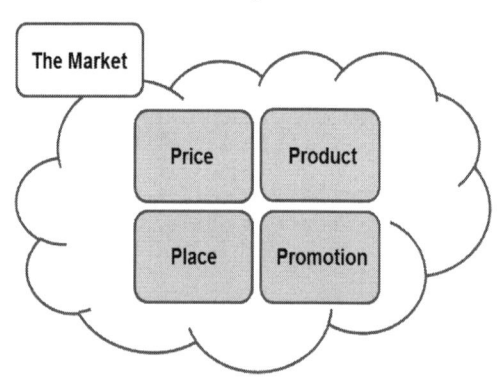

Failure to get the marketing right, and the organisation faces losses related to lost investment and potentially excess inventory, as well as opportunity losses as it could have been undertaking other profitable activities instead.

Positive Views on Model	Negative Views on Model
• Simple and established concept • Works well in FMCG and well-established markets • Good in markets where price is a dominant factor	• A PUSH not a PULL strategy • Low consideration of demand levels in the market • Poor with bespoke products or services

Price & Market Analysis

64. Porter Competitive Advantage Model

The Porter Competitive Advantage Model(1980) suggests that for an organisation to succeed, it needs to have one of three core strategies: 1) Cost Leadership, 2) Differentiation of product or service, or 3) Specific Focus on some aspect often a niche or market segment.

The Porter Competitive Advantage Model examines the strategies which are most likely to be successful in a certain type of market. Porter suggested three main strategies: Cost Leadership, Differentiation or Focus. Porter's view was that organisations which did not adopt one of these, would get "stuck in the middle", unable to make optimum profits, leaving them unable to invest, and vulnerable to the pull of obscurity and decline.

Porter identified that the choice of strategy is determined by two core factors, the competitive scope in the market and the number of sources or suppliers available.

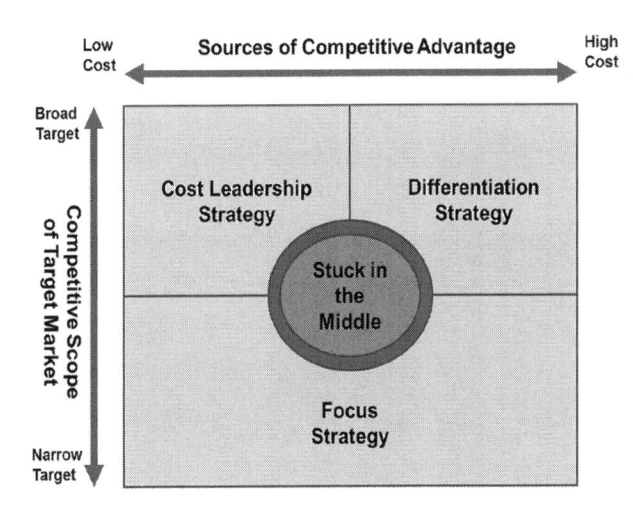

Consider the airline industry, this Porter model might include: Ryanair as a cost leader; Emirates as a differentiated quality airline; and Loganair as an airline which focuses on niche routes to remote off-shore islands around the UK.

Positive Views on Model	Negative Views on Model
• Highly reputable and long established	• The three strategies are very generic

65. Porter Five Force Model

The Porter Five Force Model is an established model used to consider forces that affect the competitiveness of a market. These include the competition in the current market, the impact of new market entrants and alternative products, as well as pressure from buyers and suppliers.

The Porter Five Force model (1980) considers the amount of demand that may be in the existing market, and how that may be affected by:

- The Competitive Rivalry of the existing companies in the market as they fight for the demand that exists;
- The impact of the customer base (Buyers) and aspects such as earnings, changes in taste, the economic outlook and taxation;
- The pressures that Suppliers can exert in the market by raising or lowering prices, or changing the supply of product into the market;
- The impact that a New Entrant (or departing competitor) has on the market and the barriers which prevent entering or leaving the market;
- The impact Substitute solutions will have on demand in the market, especially if it is underpinned by legislation, cost or technology.

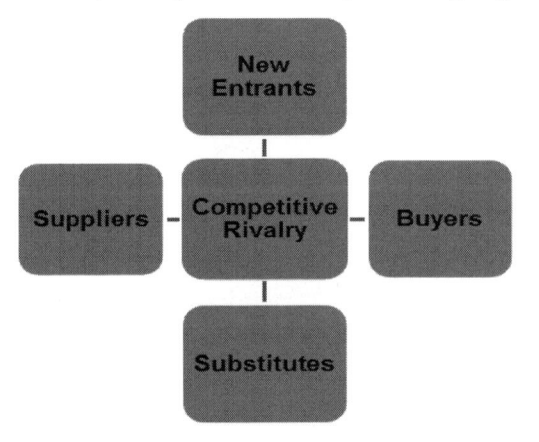

Since 1985, and the original publication, a sixth force has been identified, that of complementary products which may affect demand, for example the price of fuel in the car market.

Positive Views on Model	Negative Views on Model
• Highly reputable and long-established model • Can be adapted to reflect real numbers	• Identifying the full extent of the forces can be an issue and they can change quickly. • Doesn't consider issues like geography or political pressure

Price & Market Analysis

66. Supply Market Analysis

Supply Market Analysis is used to position suppliers in the market relative to their cost and quality. This is useful when examining an organisation and it supports the formation or analysis of a supplier strategy.

The Supply Market Analysis can be used to help position suppliers in their market based on their relative quality and cost offerings. It helps ensure that the product mix of an organisation covers the intended client base, budget or quality aspiration, and can prevent different brands from competing unnecessarily amongst themselves. Quality is however very subjective, so endeavour to use multiple opinions to reduce "Group Think" – consider the example below.

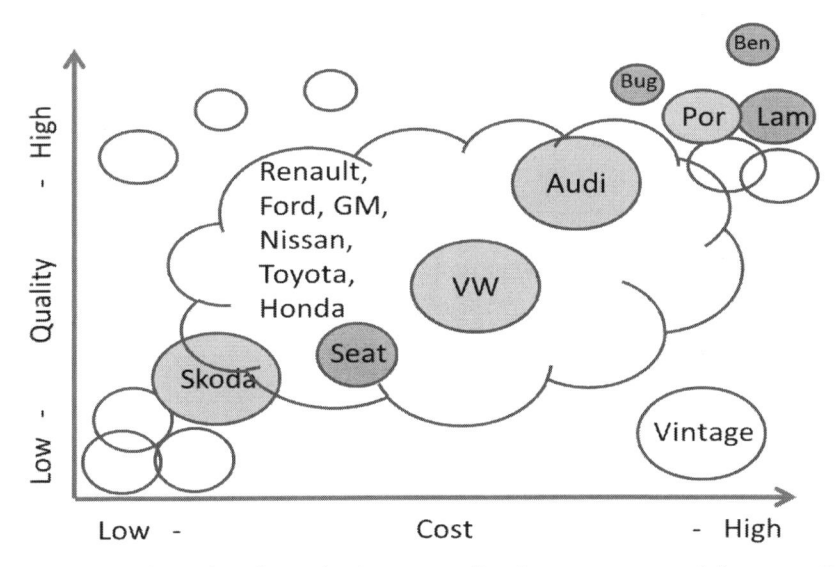

Considering the mix of products a supplier has can reveal the supplier's strategy, although some organisations actively allow their relative brands to operate in an autonomous way without cross fertilisation of ideas or strategy, perceiving internal competition to be both healthy and beneficial.

Positive Views on Model	Negative Views on Model
• Clearly shows product and market strategy when applied • Helps understand how segment coverage is developing	• What is shown may not be what the company intended • Definition of quality can be very subjective

Procurement

67. Carter 10C Model
68. Crocker Simplified Service Gap Model
69. Five Rights of Purchasing
70. Iron Triangle Model
71. Kraljic Matrix
72. Maturity Assessment Model
73. Monczka MSU Model
74. Steele & Court Supplier Preferencing Model
75. Syson Positioning Graph - Strategic Policies
75a Syson Positioning Graph - Strategic Performance

67. Carter 10C Model

The Carter 10C Model is an internationally renowned model that is used to assess suppliers prior to contract award, and can be used thereafter to assess the Supplier performance once service is underway.

The Carter 10C Model is a highly recognised model for the assessment of potential suppliers in a tender situation. The model incorporates weighting to allow the assessment to accurately balance the importance of the factors being measured with the quality of the evidence used to underpin the analysis. The Cs of each measured facet are as follows:

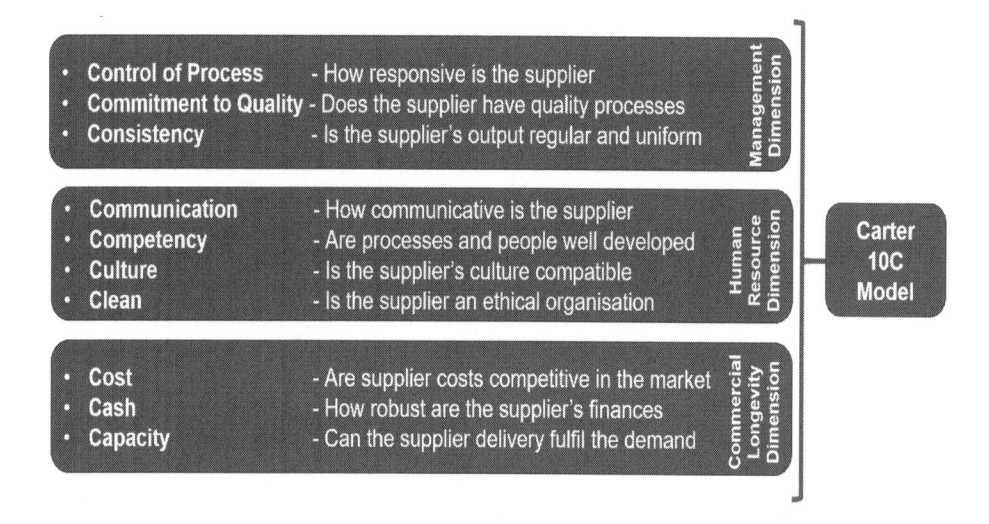

Management Dimension
- Control of Process — How responsive is the supplier
- Commitment to Quality — Does the supplier have quality processes
- Consistency — Is the supplier's output regular and uniform

Human Resource Dimension
- Communication — How communicative is the supplier
- Competency — Are processes and people well developed
- Culture — Is the supplier's culture compatible
- Clean — Is the supplier an ethical organisation

Commercial Longevity Dimension
- Cost — Are supplier costs competitive in the market
- Cash — How robust are the supplier's finances
- Capacity — Can the supplier delivery fulfil the demand

→ Carter 10C Model

Each contractor is measured based on the agreed weighting and reflecting the quality of the evidence. The scores are then multiplied together to generate an overall score for the potential supplier. The same model can then be used through the contract to measure the same facets during the life of the contract.

Positive Views on Model	Negative Views on Model
• Reflects critical areas of supplier analysis • Enables evidence and risk to be incorporated in the analysis • Facilitates weighting of facets	• Debate on the number (7,8,9 or 10) of Cs • No clear definition of some of the Cs, e.g. Communication, Customer, CSR, Compliance

68. Crocker Simplified Service Gap Model

The Crocker Simplified Service Gap Model looks at the causes of gaps in services provision between customer expectations, actual service delivery and the customer perception of the service experience.

Understanding the causes of customer dis-satisfaction is essential to an organisation and its ability to gain and maintain customers over a sustained period. The Crocker Simplified Service Gap Model looks at two distinct gaps within the service provision that generate the mismatch between service expectation and service perception.

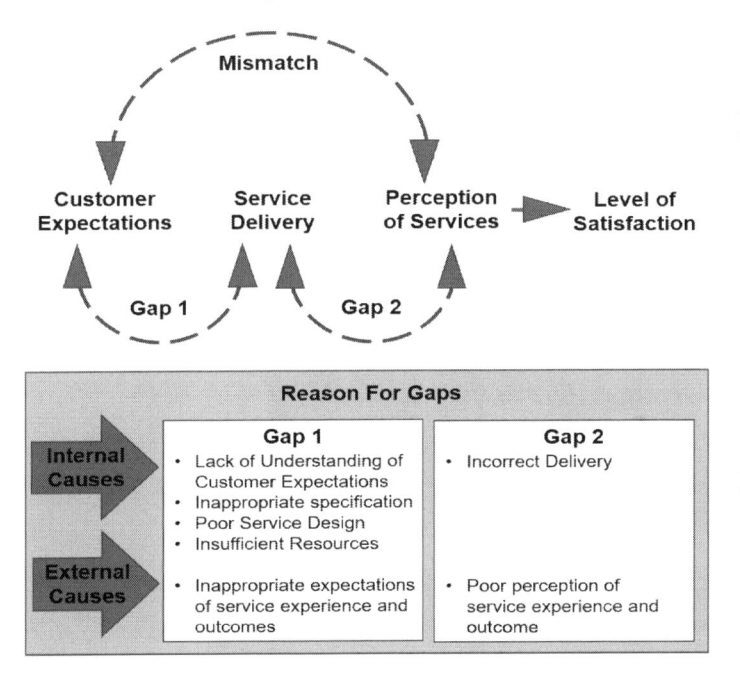

```
        Mismatch
Customer    Service      Perception      Level of
Expectations Delivery    of Services     Satisfaction
         Gap 1         Gap 2
```

	Reason For Gaps	
	Gap 1	**Gap 2**
Internal Causes	• Lack of Understanding of Customer Expectations • Inappropriate specification • Poor Service Design • Insufficient Resources	• Incorrect Delivery
External Causes	• Inappropriate expectations of service experience and outcomes	• Poor perception of service experience and outcome

From Crocker, B. *Excellence in Services Procurement* (Cambridge Academic)

Once the two gaps have been identified solutions can be implemented to resolve either the communication from the customer to the producer, or to the operational activities to improve the quality of the output to ensure it meets the customer requirements.

Positive Views on Model	Negative Views on Model
• Clearly shows where the service fails	• Assumes no third-party interference in the delivery

69. Five Rights of Purchasing

The Rights of Purchasing concept is a core element of effective procurement. The Five Rights clarify what the buyer is entitled to expect when signing a contract or placing a purchase order.

The Five Rights of Purchasing highlight very succinctly what the buyer should anticipate when agreeing a deal with a supplier.

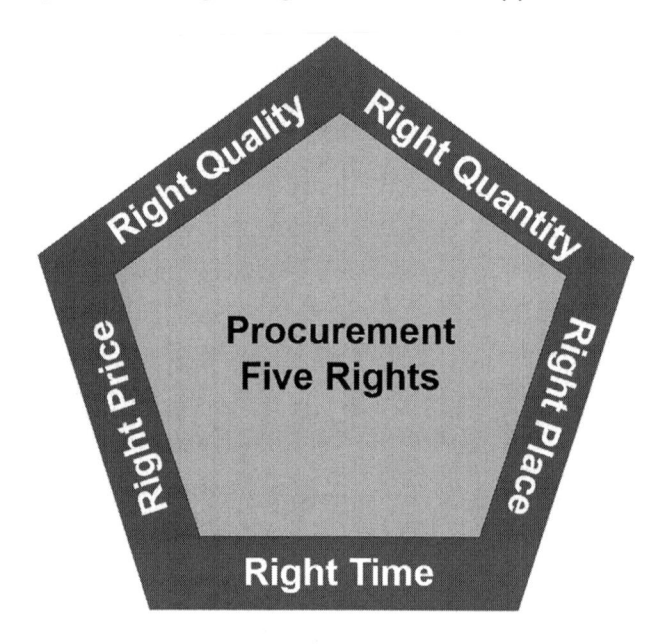

Pentagon diagram labelled with: Right Quality, Right Quantity, Right Place, Right Time, Right Price — surrounding "Procurement Five Rights".

It is not unreasonable that the buyer receives goods or services which meet the specification and are of the Right Quality, that these are supplied in the Right Quantity required and stated on the purchase order, and delivered to the Right Place as indicated.

This delivery should also occur at the Right Time stated or within a reasonable time commensurate with the prevailing circumstances, and should be at an agreed Right Price. This price should be a total price including delivery, and any extras.

Positive Views on Model	Negative Views on Model
• Helps a buyer determine if they have been fairly treated • Clearly identifies what a buyer can expect from a supplier	• Does not address a bad decision nor eliminate poor value for money or an inappropriate specification

Procurement

70. Iron Triangle Model

The Iron Triangle Model looks at the relationship between Quality, Time and Cost in a project or contract activity. It is a triple constraint model, with each of the three dynamics – Quality (Specification), Time and Cost – interdependent with a change in one having a consequential change on at least one of the others.

The Iron Triangle Model considers the relationship between Quality, (Specification), Time and Cost (although it has been used in a number of other scenarios most notably political structures) and recognises that the three dynamics directly impact on the others in a project or contract activity. For example, in a contract, the delivery of the desired Scope or Specification could be done "faster", however there would be a consequential impact with either the Cost rising (perhaps due to overtime being required) or a drop in Quality levels as the production had been rushed.

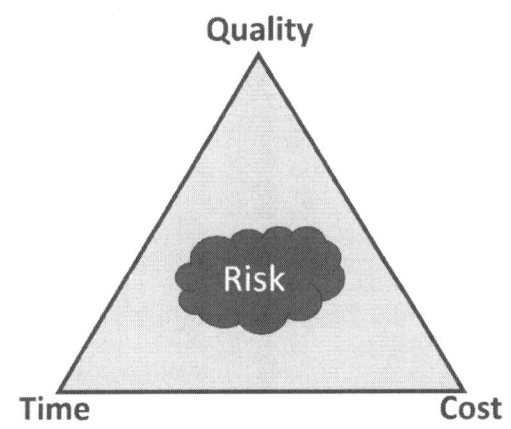

Similarly, if Quality needs to be improved, invariably Cost will rise, it will take longer, or the specification will not be as good. The Iron triangle merely aims to highlight this inter-relation.

Positive Views on Model	Negative Views on Model
• Easy to understand dynamic to highlight the symbiotic relationships and inter-dependency	• Purely an illustrative model with no demonstrable outcomes.

71. Kraljic Matrix

The Kraljic Matrix is an internationally recognised four box model which analyses the interrelation (from the buyer's perspective) between value and risk, although a number of variants do exist. Each box refers to a type of relationship, these being: Strategic, Bottleneck, Non-Critical and Leverage.

The Kraljic Matrix (1983) examines the relationship between value and risk although some texts have different axis titles. An organisation may use this as part of its segmentation process to position contracts or procurement relationships. The model helps identify strategic characteristics of an item, for example, a bottleneck item which would need special consideration as the buying relationship would be restrictive.

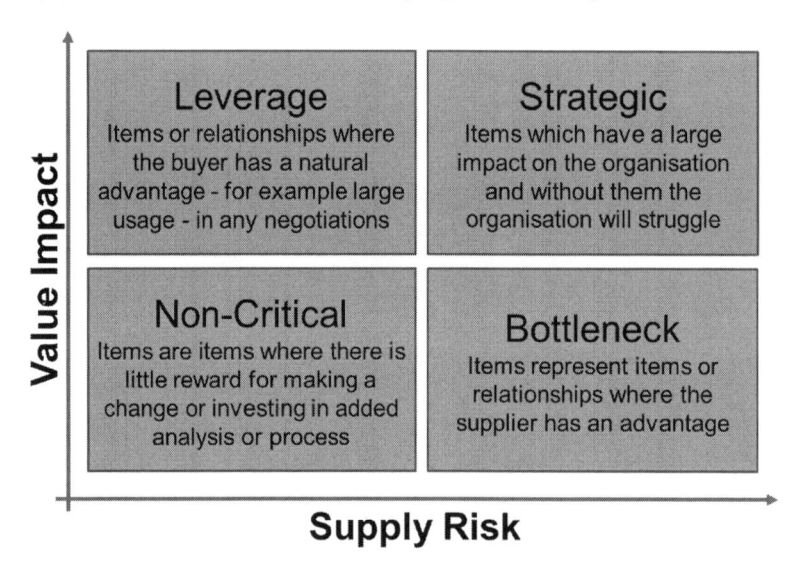

Value Impact ↑

Leverage	Strategic
Items or relationships where the buyer has a natural advantage - for example large usage - in any negotiations	Items which have a large impact on the organisation and without them the organisation will struggle
Non-Critical	Bottleneck
Items are items where there is little reward for making a change or investing in added analysis or process	Items represent items or relationships where the supplier has an advantage

Supply Risk →

Note: Consider these perspectives in conjunction with the Steele & Court Supplier Preferencing Model (see Model 74) as it needs to tie in with the supplier's perspective – you may deem a facet of your procurement to be mission critical but the supplier may see you as a nuisance and have no motivation to form a relationship between the two organisations.

Positive Views on Model	Negative Views on Model
• Very commonly used and recognised model • Simple matrix and clear	• Lots of different variants • Cost not considered directly in the model • Can lack precision

Procurement

72. Maturity Assessment Model

The Maturity Assessment Model was developed to provide a collaborative profile for an organisation. It provides a benchmark and development profile to be used for internal assessment for the buying organisation or as an initial profile of potential collaborative partners.

The Maturity Assessment Model assesses three key variables: Attributes, Abilities and Attitudes, with the target being an optimum score of four in each, representing an effective and integrated collaboration.

Maturity Assessment

The maturity matrix provides a platform against which organisations can review their internal development needs.

	Attributes	Ability	Attitude
A	Operational processes are well defined and integrate collaborative approaches	There is a high level of experience at all levels focused on effective collaboration	There is clear corporate commitment and leadership that cascades throughout the operations
B	There is limited application of shared processes and performance indicators	There are individuals at various levels that have demonstrable skills in collaboration	There is evidence of successful individual collaborative programmes in effect
C	There are robust internal processes and performance indicators	There is appreciation of collaborative approaches but a lack of skills	There is appreciation at the operating level of the value of effective relationships
D	Operates with a traditional contract and procedural based approach	No appreciation of a practical approach to the value of relationships	Only operates a robust and effective arms length contracting approach

Accordingly it is an important tool to be used when implementing BS11000 /ISO44001 the standard for Collaborative Business Relationships. A note of caution however, it is vital to ensure consistency and objectivity when scoring in order to provide a factual and accurate view of the relationship.

Positive Views on Model	Negative Views on Model
• Gives consistent framework for Buyer assessment • Good for consistency and audit	• Assessment might be subjective which would undermine the results

73. Monczka MSU Model

The Monczka MSU Model analyses each step in the procurement process with the aim of improving the strategic procurement performance, efficiency and effectiveness of the organisation.

The model was conceived at Michigan State University by Dr Robert Monczka (can be called the MSU Model) and often compared with Kraljic. It systematically addresses each stage of the organisation's procurement process. As each step is considered, it is analysed, audited and mapped to give a clear understanding of its objective. Monczka suggested that there are 8 different strategic processes which can be seen, these are:

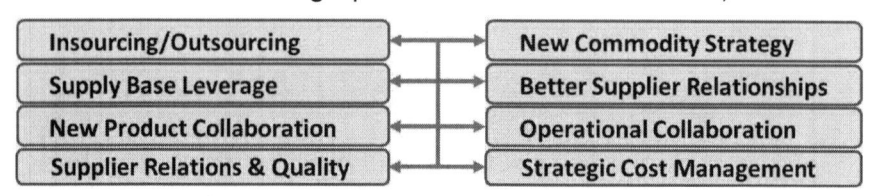

Insourcing/Outsourcing	New Commodity Strategy
Supply Base Leverage	Better Supplier Relationships
New Product Collaboration	Operational Collaboration
Supplier Relations & Quality	Strategic Cost Management

1. **Insourcing/Outsourcing** – Is the activity a core competency of the organisation?
2. **Development of commodity strategies** – Do the commodities have specific needs or requirements?
3. **Leverage of a world class supply base** – Is the supply base effective, best of breed, challenged and stretched?
4. **Development and management of supplier relationships** – Are win-win, trusting relationships in place with the core suppliers?
5. **Supplier collaboration with new product development** – Is there Early Supplier Involvement (ESI) in the R&D or marketing teams?
6. **Supplier collaboration in operation and final delivery process** – Are suppliers involved in the whole Supply Chain with aspects such as ESI, VMI or symbiotic initiatives?
7. **Quality and supplier development** – Is there dialogue with suppliers over quality and performance improvements?
8. **Strategic cost management** – Are costs managed and appropriate across the Supply Chain, are cost reduction processes in place?

Positive Views on Model	Negative Views on Model
• A systematic, analytical and structured model • Based on best practice	• May not apply to all organisations, for example the public sector

74. Steele & Court Supplier Preferencing Model

The Steele & Court (1996) Supplier Preferencing Model is used to examine the view a supplier may have of a customer. This is often utilised by the customer to understand how valued its business is to a supplier or to evaluate what strategy the supplier has adopted towards it.

Whilst the Kraljic Model (See Model 71) is useful for understanding the prevailing risk and reward dynamic in relation to a supplier, it is not unreasonable to suppose that a supplier would have a similar view of the buying organisation. The Steele & Court(1996) Supplier Preferencing Model in a contract setting is useful for assessing what this perspective may be and helps when determining the strategy taken by the suppliers to an organisation, be they a nonchalant supplier, or indeed a supplier for whom your organisation is seen as core.

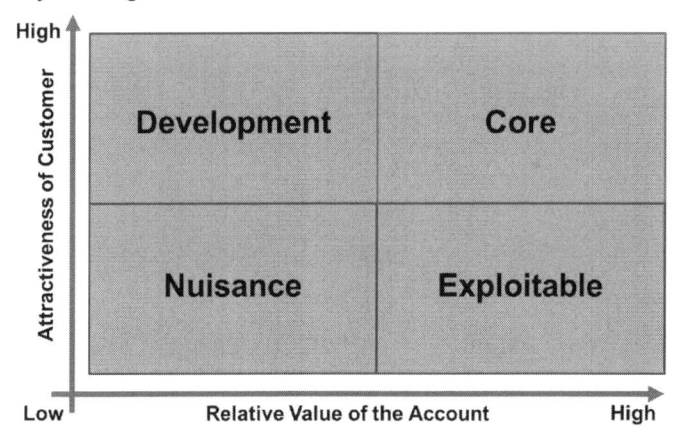

	Low Relative Value of the Account	High
High Attractiveness of Customer	Development	Core
Low	Nuisance	Exploitable

Understanding these different perspectives is important. A supplier perceiving you as a "Nuisance" customer will have a very different approach than one who sees you as "Core". This can lead to issues where the different parties have a conflicting view or allow commercial opportunities to be missed and has clear parallels with the Kraljic Matrix which looks at the alternative perspective i.e. the Buyer's view of the Supplier.

Positive Views on Model	Negative Views on Model
• Well known and understood four box model • Simple to apply and understand	• No specific direction on remedial actions

75. Syson Positioning Graph – Strategic Policies

The Syson Positioning Model illustrates the relationship between the Procurement activity and its evolution from an efficient transactional activity to a proactive, effective function within the organisation.

Syson saw the Procurement function divided into three main areas of focus: transaction, commercial and proactive. The more developed the Procurement activity, the greater its involvement in commercial and strategic activities and the more involved Procurement becomes in commercial and strategic activities the greater its return of investment.

Positioning Graph = Strategies / Policies

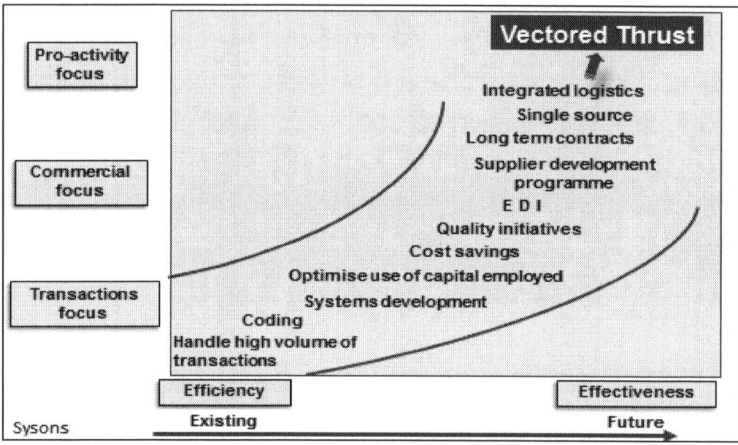

[Graph: Y-axis shows Pro-activity focus, Commercial focus, Transactions focus (bottom to top). X-axis shows Efficiency (Existing) to Effectiveness (Future). Curve labeled "Vectored Thrust" passes through: Handle high volume of transactions, Coding, Systems development, Optimise use of capital employed, Cost savings, Quality initiatives, EDI, Supplier development programme, Long term contracts, Single source, Integrated logistics. Source: Sysons]

(Cited in Bailey, P., Farmer, D., Crocker, B., et al (2015) *Procurement, Principles and Management*)

Syson viewed that Procurement has been transformed from a service function with aims expressed by price, quality and delivery to one which makes a contribution to sustainable competitive advantage by reducing the cost of ownership, cycle time reduction and improving time to market, moving from being efficient to being effective and aiming for proactivity.

Positive Views on Model	Negative Views on Model
• Provides useful Procurement road-map or pathway • Highlights ideas and opportunities	• Lacks detail as to how this may be achieved

Procurement

75a. Syson Positioning Graph – Strategic Performance

The Syson Model, in addition to highlighting the various activities, strategies and directions that a procurement function should endeavour to embrace, highlights the various measures of performance that should be introduced to measure and manage the transitional activity.

The Syson Strategies and Policies detailed in Model 75 were assigned to individual KPI indicators and measurement criteria to ensure that each aspect was driven forward to generate the best commercial return from the developing operational activity resulting in the Syson Measures of Performance Graph as shown below:

Positioning Graph - Measures of Performance

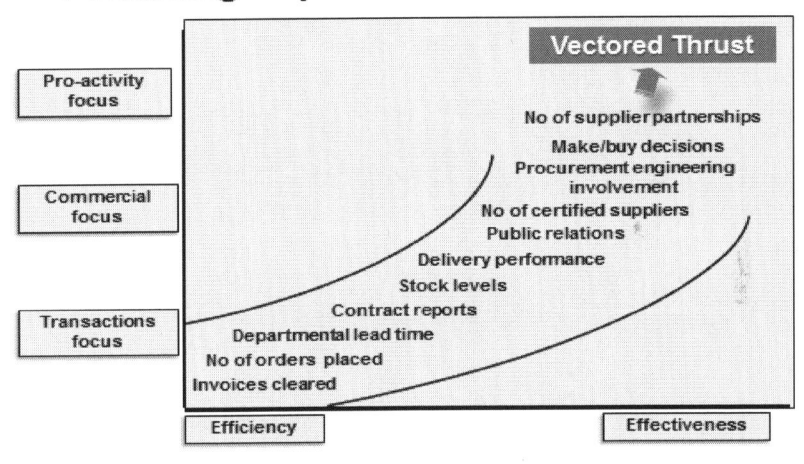

```
                                        Vectored Thrust
                                              ↑
  Pro-activity
    focus
                              No of supplier partnerships
                              Make/buy decisions
                              Procurement engineering
                                    involvement
  Commercial                  No of certified suppliers
    focus                     Public relations
                         Delivery performance
                         Stock levels
                      Contract reports
  Transactions      Departmental lead time
    focus           No of orders placed
                   Invoices cleared

        Efficiency                        Effectiveness
```

Whilst a subset of the main Syson Model, this secondary element highlights the aspects of a business that can benefit from the Syson transition, each with demonstrable benefit and clear metrics for the organisation to assess and manage development against.

Positive Views on Model	Negative Views on Model
• Highlights clear operational benefits • Introduces a measure or KPI against each operational opportunity	• The KPI measures are only a suggested few with many others existing • KPI measures address generic rather than bespoke opportunities

Quality

76. Cost of Poor Quality (COPQ) Model
77. Deming / Shewhart Plan-Do-Check-Act (PDCA)
78. EFQM Excellence Model
79. Fishbone / Root Cause Analysis / Ishikawa Diagram
80. Kaizen
81. Six Sigma, DMAIC & SIPOC Models
82. Voice of the Customer & Quality Circles

76. Cost of Poor Quality (COPQ) Model

The Cost of Poor Quality Model is a standard operations management measure and an integral part of the Six Sigma analysis; it evaluates the effective total cost and impact of a quality issue on the organisation's performance.

The Cost of Poor Quality Model is used to identify the total cost and implication associated with a quality failure. The concept is used to justify the investment in quality and support the preparation of a realistic business case underpinned with a quantifiable benefit.

Calculating the COPQ requires a broad assessment of the repercussions associated with a quality issue, these may include:

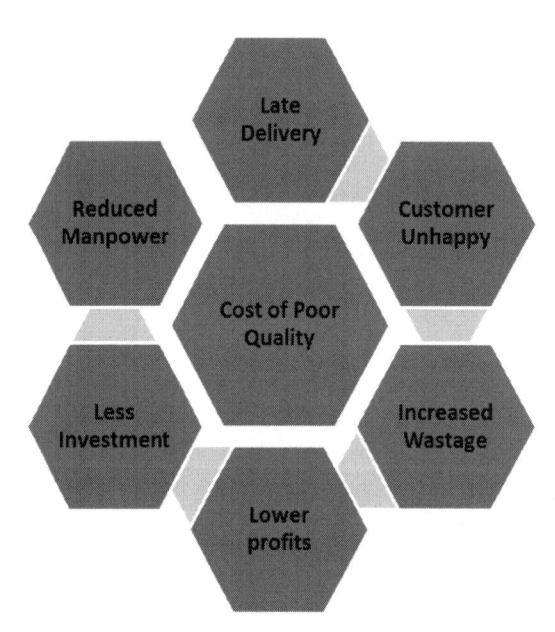

- Lost Sales & Profit
- Supplier Relationship
- Reputation Loss
- Defects
- Motivation
- Disputes
- Waste Materials
- Downtime
- Customer Delays
- Inspection Costs
- Rework
- Warranty

Surrounding "Cost of Poor Quality": Late Delivery, Customer Unhappy, Increased Wastage, Lower profits, Less Investment, Reduced Manpower.

Positive Views on Model	Negative Views on Model
• Highlights the positive implications of managing quality • Considers total cost as opposed to issues like customer perception and PR	• No direct measurement of cost • Does not directly suggest how remediation should be undertaken

77. Deming / Shewhart Plan-Do-Check-Act (PDCA)

The Shewhart Plan-Do-Check-Act (PDCA) process is a fundamental part of a Total Quality Management (TQM) approach popularised by Deming and an integrated part of the Six Sigma concept. It ensures a structured and systematic approach to making process and quality improvements.

The Deming / Shewhart Plan-Do-Check-Act process (sometimes referred to as a wheel or cycle) is commonly adopted by businesses looking to implement and control change in processes to improve quality or efficiency.

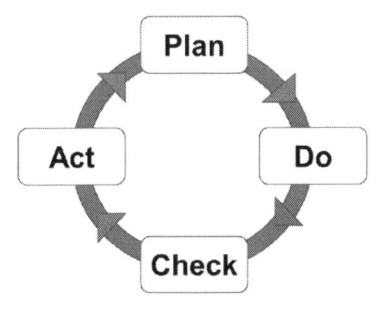

The **Plan** action assesses a problem, finds the root cause and identifies the outputs that are required from the process.

The **Do** action is responsible for implementing the Plan.

The **Check** action verifies the change, compares actual with projected results and ensures that the change has been successful.

The **Act** action addresses any issues or deviations identified by the Check action to enable the process change to be adopted.

Note: Sometimes this model is distorted for example Act can be Adjust, Plan can be Prepare, Do can be Deliver, and in some variants, there is a preceding O for observation.

Positive Views on Model	Negative Views on Model
• Strong, well-used model • Works well with Continuous Improvement, and with radical or incremental change	• Needs management support • Maybe viewed as a statistical model which can alienate some users

78. EFQM Excellence Model

The EFQM Excellence Model is a quality management model developed by the European Foundation for Quality Management and is used to benchmark the proficiency and quality of an organisation based against a clear and recognised set of metrics.

The objective of the EFQM organisation is to drive quality improvements through the rigorous and regular assessment process based upon the model and its underpinning framework. The model runs through a systematic assessment audit, enabling clear identification of areas for improvement and focuses on eight areas of corporate excellence.

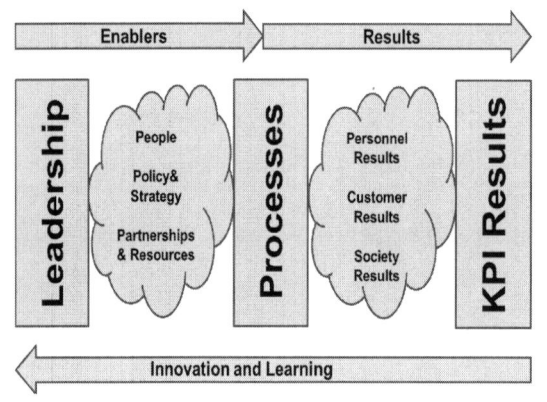

Eight Areas of Excellence

- Added customer value
- Improved vision
- Higher performance
- Enhanced leadership
- Improved innovation
- Staff more motivated
- Results more reliable

Diagram: Enablers → Results; Leadership → (People, Policy & Strategy, Partnerships & Resources) → Processes → (Personnel Results, Customer Results, Society Results) → KPI Results; Innovation and Learning feedback loop.

Much of the process analysis, data collection and performance reviews are undertaken by internal operatives through self-assessment and peer observation enabling the organisation to operate and police the process using internal resources.

Using internal operatives enables a higher degree of ownership, and helps buy-in when issues need resolving, giving more effective and innovative solutions and improved team understanding.

Positive Views on Model	Negative Views on Model
• Customer and objective driven • Drives continuous improvement • Works in most organisations including public sector • Sets standards and manages corporate targets	• Self-assessment needs to be carefully monitored • Organisation needs to ensure complete buy-in • Prone to manipulation of findings and outputs

Quality

79. Fishbone/Root Cause Analysis/ Ishikawa Diagram

The Fishbone or Ishikawa Diagram(1960) is used to breakdown an issue into its component parts to allow identification of the possible root-causes of the issue thereafter assisting in the generation of a solution. Issue is traditionally quality related, but may be any problem identified.

The Fishbone or Ishikawa diagram breaks an issue – for example a quality issue – into its core components allowing an easier identification of the root-cause of the problem and possible solutions. When conceived, the model had four core bones, however it has evolved into six categories (or 6M's) in the modern Fishbone diagram, these are: Machinery, Man, Method, Mother Nature, Measurement and Materials. The example below suggests reasons why a café has started to produce cold coffee:

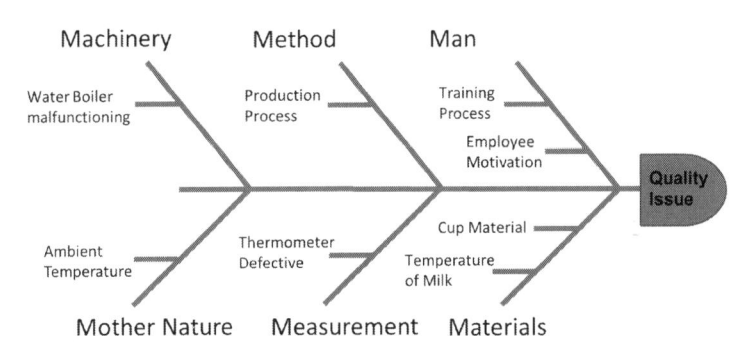

The six categories cover every element that could be present, the Mother Nature bone capturing nature, climate and Force Majeure aspects that were hitherto difficult to categorise. Once the possibilities have been identified, cross-functional brainstorming is used to subdivide ideas ready to be verified or eliminated as root-causes of the issue in question.

Positive Views on Model	Negative Views on Model
• Good for breaking issues into possible root-causes • Enables a possible cause to be broken down further to better identify the cause	• Needs effective cross-functional brainstorming to generate the bones • Can produce too many options which take time and money to evaluate/eliminate • Other "bones" often used

80. Kaizen

Kaizen is a Japanese philosophy usually associated with Toyota where continuous improvement and positive proactive change is encouraged to address issues identified by the workforce within the organisation.

Kaizen was introduced into Japan after the 1950's by Deming during the reconstruction of the Japanese economy, and was embraced by the organisations and people involved, most notably Toyota.

The concept of Kaizen is to introduce positive, proactive change in a structured and stable manner, driven from within by the workforce, with the change taking manageable, often small steps to avoid major upheaval and to ensure cross functional buy-in and support. Core to the concept is the need for continuous change driven by the internal stakeholders; the underpinning philosophy of Kaizen is that perfection is a utopia which should be aimed for, but that opportunities to improve will always be present.

Kaizen is particularly focused on developing a smooth-running, stable structure, minimising waste, and ensuring the highest quality of output with the lowest risk to the operation. These concepts were developed in depth by Toyota with their 3M waste concept – Mura, Muri & Muda – i.e. No waste, smooth flow without irregularities. A focus on elimination of waste and improvement in Quality (the wrong quality being seen as a waste, noting over-engineering or excessively high quality for which the producer is not paid is also a waste) within every activity is a clear objective, with use of aspects such as Quality Circles, Voice of the Customer, Six Sigma, JIT, Kanban's, automation and other techniques to identify opportunities.

The implementation of Kaizen is often undertaken with a Deming Plan-Do-Check-Act approach (See Model 77) to ensure a smooth, measured and calculated transition with a feedback and verification loop incorporated.

Positive Views on Model	Negative Views on Model
• Well-established and recognised approach to change • Incorporates employee buy-in	• Approach needs cross organisation commitment • Can be time-consuming

Quality

81. Six Sigma Concept, DMAIC & SIPOC Models

Six Sigma is a quality theory intended to reduce defects to less than 3.4 defects in a million units produced. The process uses statistical methods, established models and specific processes to identify where and how quality issues occur enabling their remedy. Use of SIPOC to break a Supply Chain down and the DMAIC (Define-Measure-Analyse-Improve-Control) concept to remedy issues are two such models.

The Six Sigma concept is used by many organisations to drive quality processes and improvements through the organisation. It is considered by such organisations as a way of life, with process embedded in the core ethos of the management and operation. Sceptics of Six Sigma suggest it is too heavily reliant upon statistical and mathematical analysis however there are many non-mathematical concepts contained within that address the procedures and structure of how the organisation works.

For example, the tool used to analyse the Supply Chain considers it over five elements as shown below and merely aims to break down the Supply Chain into manageable pieces:

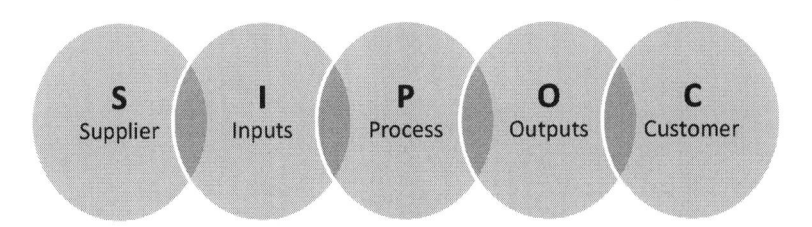

S Supplier — **I** Inputs — **P** Process — **O** Outputs — **C** Customer

Equally, the DMAIC approach (Design-Measure-Analyse-Improve-Control) is used to create structure when addressing quality defects and reformation of the operating processes.

Positive Views on Model	Negative Views on Model
• Very structured and established approach • Underpinned with statistical data and analysis	• Mathematical and often difficult to understand • Needs specially trained people and be built into the organisation's culture

82. Voice of the Customer & Quality Circles

The Voice of the Customer (VOC) and Quality Circles are simple concepts within the Six-Sigma process used to understand, engage and capture ideas from both external and internal stakeholders within an organisation, helping drive improvement and quality based on real issues.

The Voice of the Customer (VOC) process is used to encourage both internal and external "customers" to think about and document ideas that could lead to process enhancement, cost saving, waste reduction, quality improvements and other positive changes to the operation. The VOC process is a relatively simple one; participants are asked to identify any ideas or issues which they believe would lead to a service, profit or quality improvement. Ideas are reviewed leading to a categorised set of potential improvement projects.

Voice of the Customer

- Request Customer Input
- Collect Customer Ideas
- Collate and Evaluate Ideas
- Prioritise and Shortlist Ideas
- Develop Delivery Teams
- Assess and Trial Potential Changes
- Implement Changes
- Review Changes and Adjust

The Quality Circles concept originated in the 1960s and is a powerful way of engaging staff into Quality and Continuous Improvement projects. It forms an essential part of a normal Total Quality Management process, and is commonly used within Six-Sigma projects as well, often aligned with the VOC (Voice of the Customer) approach. The teams are cross-functional, multi-skilled and participation is often voluntary although unpaid, and not required to operate to any specific, pre-agreed format or agenda.

Positive Views on Model	Negative Views on Model
• Simple to implement • Engages customers, staff and stakeholders	• Results can be unreliable • Takes time and investment

Relationships & Stakeholder Management

83. Burnes & New Customer/Supplier Relationships
84. Cox Supplier Relationships Management Model
85. Crocker Managing Satisfaction of Service Quality Model
86. Customer-Supplier Partnership Bridge
87. Egan Stakeholder Positioning (Labels) Model
88. Johnson Supplier Management Behaviours Model
89. Mendelow Matrix
90. Relationship Determination Model
91. Stakeholder Allegiance Matrix
92. Supplier Relationship Management (SRM) Interfaces
93. Thomas & Kilmann Conflict Mode Instrument

83. Burnes & New Customer/Supplier Relationships

The Burnes & New Customer/Supplier Relationships Model examines the issue of cost and benefit secured by the buyer and the supplier in collaborative approaches within Procurement and Supply Chain activities.

The Burnes & New Customer/Supplier Relationships Model depicts the contentious issue of imbalances between the distribution of costs and benefits from a collaborative approach. Evidence suggests that the benefits appear easier to achieve than is often the case. The research which underpins the model highlights the imbalance in the costs and benefits of various initiatives, shown below:

Customer/Supplier Relationships

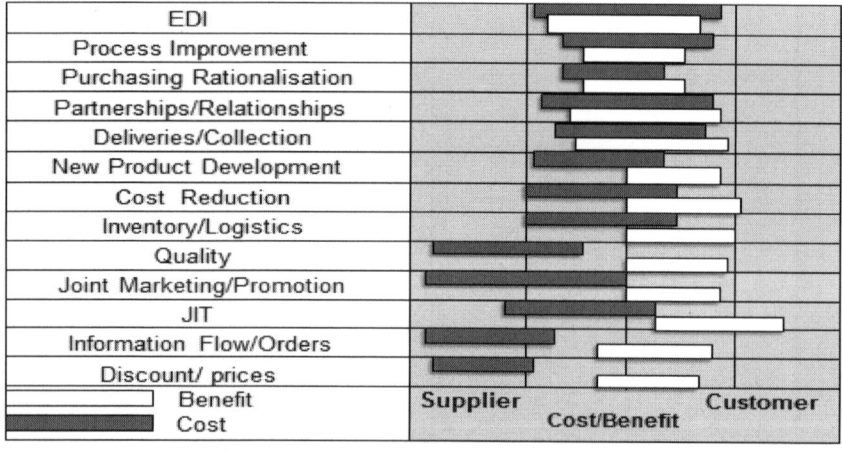

Initiative	
EDI	
Process Improvement	
Purchasing Rationalisation	
Partnerships/Relationships	
Deliveries/Collection	
New Product Development	
Cost Reduction	
Inventory/Logistics	
Quality	
Joint Marketing/Promotion	
JIT	
Information Flow/Orders	
Discount/ prices	

Legend: Benefit / Cost — Supplier ← Cost/Benefit → Customer

New.S, Burnes.B (1998) Developing effective customer supply relationships IJQRM

Burnes & New suggest that a win-lose outcome is often masked by an aura of collaboration with some findings showing a predominance of costs borne by the supplier (rather than shared) with the costs perhaps perceived as an investment by the supplier to secure longer term benefits. The implication of the model is that there appears to be a need for more of a "trust with verification approach". This model does not validate the concept of win-win, but does indicate that a more sophisticated, longer-term view of the relative costs and benefits of collaboration may need to be taken.

Positive Views on Model	Negative Views on Model
• Supported with detailed research	• Complicated and arguably very subjective

84. Cox Supplier Relationships Management Model

The Cox Supplier Relationships Management Model looks at the Buyer-Supplier relationships which are characterised by two main elements: the nature of the interaction between the two parties and the manner in which the benefits of the relationship are divided between the two parties.

The two dimensions of the model – Relationship Type and Sharing of Gain – provide us with four different generic relationship types rejecting the idea that buyer-supplier relationships adhere to neat contrasts, such as that between arm's length and collaborative interactions only. For instance, Adversarial Collaborative (such as between a large retailer and small supplier) does not provide a win-win unless there is a niche being fulfilled.

Power affects the expectation of the parties over the commercial returns that should accrue to them from the relationship and thus affects the willingness of the two parties to invest in collaborative activities. The model assists managers make relationship decisions and frame their relationship expectations around general assessments of what they think the costs and benefits will be of a particular type of interaction.

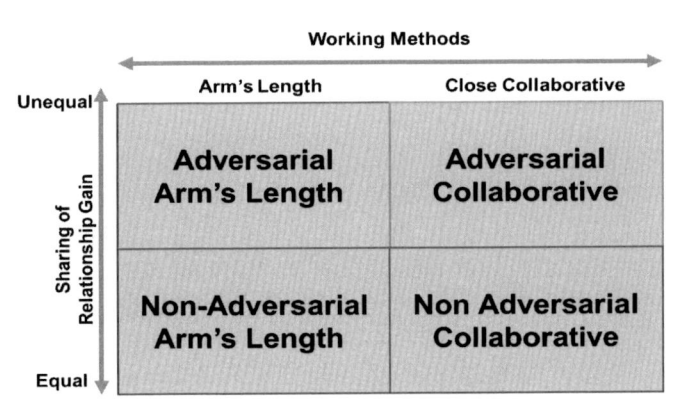

	Arm's Length	Close Collaborative
Unequal	Adversarial Arm's Length	Adversarial Collaborative
Equal	Non-Adversarial Arm's Length	Non Adversarial Collaborative

Working Methods (horizontal axis) / Sharing of Relationship Gain (vertical axis)

Cox Supplier Relationship Types

Positive Views on Model	Negative Views on Model
• Strategises the relationship and brings the opportunity and value into the corporate context.	• Terminology and similar box labels can discourage use

85. Crocker Managing Satisfaction of Service Quality

The Crocker Managing Satisfaction of Service Quality Model combines levels of expectation and zone of tolerance, with (1) the outcome of a service, (2) level of satisfaction and (3) dissatisfaction.

Procurement must be fully attuned to its internal customers and understand their perceptions of a service in order to ensure that they fully appreciate what is, and what is not, acceptable in terms of service delivery.

It looks at how expectations give way to a perceived satisfaction using the service process. An example of a maintenance service can be applied to this model using data such as response time (e.g. one hour), arrival, diagnosis, actual time taken to fix on first attempt, discussion of findings, departure; and total elapsed time for the service. Performance within the zone of tolerance results in satisfaction, if the event occurs faster it may move into the higher zone and generate delight with the customer, or take longer leading to dissatisfaction.

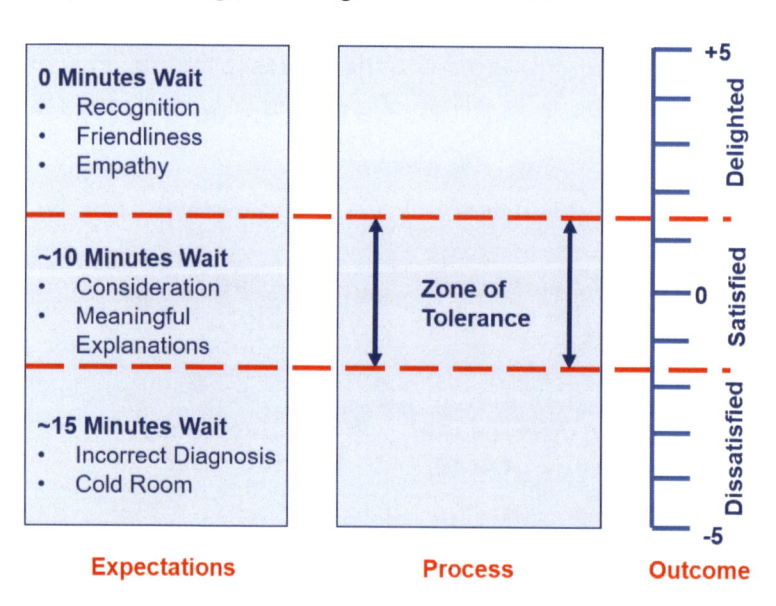

0 Minutes Wait
- Recognition
- Friendliness
- Empathy

~10 Minutes Wait
- Consideration
- Meaningful Explanations

~15 Minutes Wait
- Incorrect Diagnosis
- Cold Room

Zone of Tolerance

Scale: +5 Delighted, 0 Satisfied, -5 Dissatisfied

Expectations — **Process** — **Outcome**

Positive Views on Model	Negative Views on Model
• Aligns the concepts of expectation and satisfaction with stakeholder tolerance	• Zone of tolerance and outcome can be very subjective

86. Customer-Supplier Partnership Bridge

The Customer-Supplier Partnership Bridge is used to identify and secure the benefits derivable from more collaborative, partnership style, supplier relationships and the establishment of trust.

The Customer-Supplier Partnership Bridge provides details of the key and foundational elements necessary for achieving effective customer-supplier relationships and delivery of mutual "win-win" benefits.

Trust can be defined as "one party's belief that the other party in the relationship will not knowingly exploit its vulnerabilities with adverse opportunistic behaviours, even when such exploitation would not be detected."

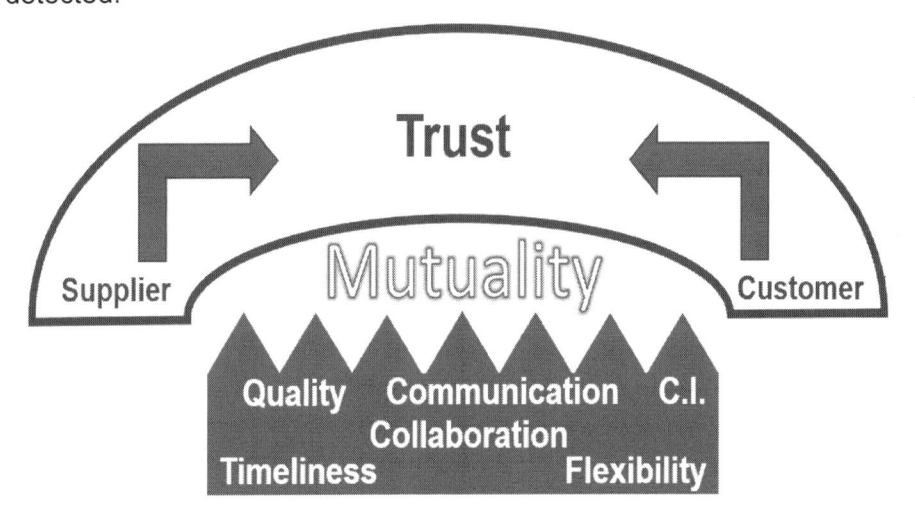

Both sides of the relationship are required to adapt their behaviours in order to ensure that these elements are capitalised upon. A major pre-requisite for the model to succeed is Continuous Improvement (CI).

Positive Views on Model	Negative Views on Model
• Clear illustrative model • Illustrates the primary issues that need to come together to generate trust in a relationship	• Culture, risk and value may also need to be considered when developing trust and mutuality • Other diverse stakeholder engagement is recommended

87. Egan Stakeholder Positioning (Labels) Model

The Egan Stakeholder Positioning Model is used to categorise and analyse stakeholders to enable a stakeholder strategy to be formulated to overcome issues which prevent change occurring seamlessly.

The Egan Stakeholder Positioning Model (sometimes called Egan's Labels) is populated with the reasons why people resist change, these include:

Fear of the unknown/surprise: This occurs when change is implemented without prior warning to the affected stakeholders, and without helping them through the process;

Mistrust: If a manager has not yet earned the trust of their employees, then mistrust of change will become apparent;

Loss of job security/control: When companies restructure or downsize it causes fear among employees that they will lose their jobs or be moved into other positions without their consent;

Bad timing: Adding too much change over a short period of time usually fails, as individuals suffer from "change fatigue";

An individual's predisposition toward change: Some people dislike change because they prefer stability, becoming suspicious of change and more likely to resist.

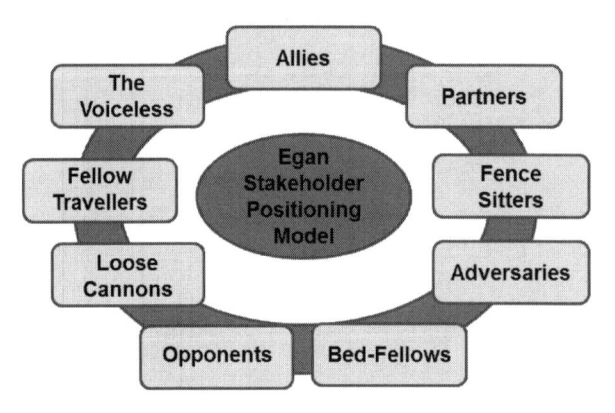

Being aware of the reasons people resist change will help you implement change with fewer issues. This model categorises but does not give remedies to risk.

Positive Views on Model	Negative Views on Model
• Identifies the specific obstacles that need to be overcome to effect change in a project	• Does not give a remedy • Labels people which can be contentious

88. Johnson Supplier Management Behaviours Model

The Johnson Supplier Management Behaviour Model looks at how effective SRM can deliver benefit through a solid supplier management approach that reflects the difficulty of the market and duration of the contract to lock in value from sourcing often lost in post-contract activity.

The Johnson Supplier Management Behaviour Model looks at client organisational behaviour towards suppliers by matching Market Difficulty with Anticipated duration of relationship or probability of re-engagement.

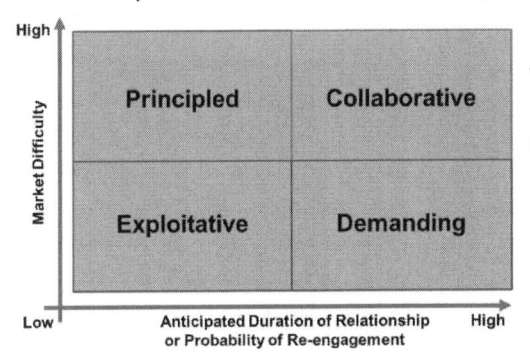

Market Difficulty High	Principled	Collaborative
Low	Exploitative	Demanding
	Anticipated Duration of Relationship or Probability of Re-engagement Low → High	

Johnson, R (2003) *Supplier Management: A deal of time and effort*

Principled There is little possibility of long-term relationships forming and few potential suppliers. A mixture of persuasion and firm negotiation is needed to develop preferred suppliers in order to leverage opportunities.

Collaboration High possibility of long-term relationships with a single source whereby both parties spend time to build trust and develop mutually beneficial interfaces.

Exploitation Limited long-term relationships, so gain maximum benefits from leverage using competition and playing the spot market.

Demanding High possibility of long-term relationships with preferred supplier status. Competition used for benchmarking purposes with buyers looking to develop closer relationships. The model is useful for categorising client behaviours but is limited by the consideration of only two variables.

Positive Views on Model	Negative Views on Model
• Focuses on relationship behaviour to add optimum value	• Only considers two variables

89. Mendelow Matrix

The Mendelow(1991) four box matrix helps identify the best strategy to adopt with different stakeholders based on the relative power of the stakeholder and the importance of the issue to the stakeholder.

The Mendelow(1991) Matrix combines the relative influence of stakeholders with their importance to a specific project. The matrix is used to understand the individual stakeholder needs and establish an appropriate strategy to ensure that they are managed appropriately.

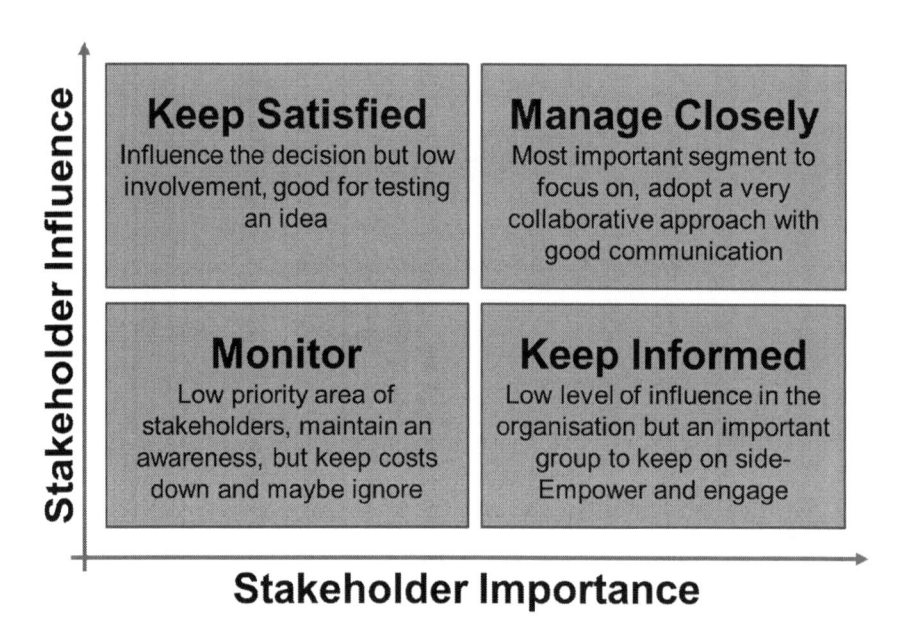

Stakeholder Influence ↑		
Keep Satisfied	Influence the decision but low involvement, good for testing an idea	**Manage Closely** — Most important segment to focus on, adopt a very collaborative approach with good communication
Monitor	Low priority area of stakeholders, maintain an awareness, but keep costs down and maybe ignore	**Keep Informed** — Low level of influence in the organisation but an important group to keep on side- Empower and engage

Stakeholder Importance →

Each stakeholder type needs to be frequently reviewed throughout the project or change activity as their individuality may result in the stakeholder's needs, status, vision or perspective shifting thus requiring the strategy to be adjusted accordingly.

Positive Views on Model	Negative Views on Model
• Helps develop stakeholder specific strategy • Helps identify stakeholder risks	• Doesn't recognise changes in stakeholder perspective • May lead to stakeholders identifying others being treated differently • Variants of the box descriptors do exist

Relationships & Stakeholder Management

90. Relationship Determination Model

The Relationship Determination Model maps a continuum of relationships dependent upon the level of commitment required, from Competitive Leverage with a minimum level of trust and commitment through to Strategic Alliance with high levels of trust and mutual commitment.

Competitive Leverage – a buyer's market with many suppliers and large client spend characterised by multiple sourcing, competitive tendering and frequent switching.

The model depicts the range of behaviours necessary to progress through the continuum.

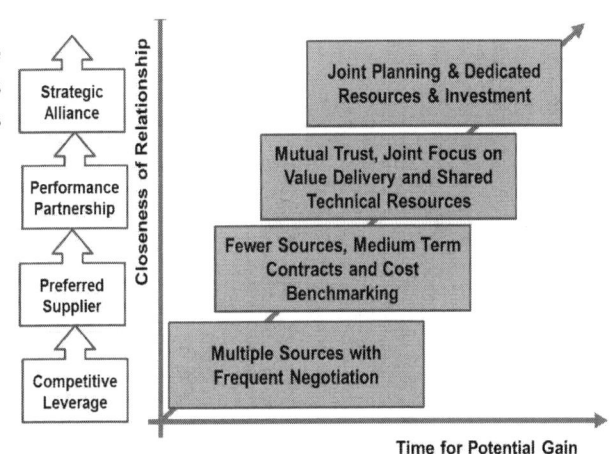

Preferred Suppliers are fewer in number and pre-qualified. For example, Toyota concentrates on structured supplier appraisal of Quality, Cost, Technical expertise and Management Capability giving improved relationships, fewer defects, reduced cycle times and faster time to market.

Performance Partnership involves a small number of suppliers for co-development. Activities include: supplier rationalisation, joint CFTs, a focus on value, a reduction of Total Cost of Ownership and a high degree of Openness and Trust.

Strategic Alliances are very small in number and are associated with co-location and co-manufacturing. In order to move along the continuum there must be an appropriate distribution of gains i.e. a win-win relationship.

Positive Views on Model	Negative Views on Model
• Clearly categorises the different levels in buyer behaviour	• Doesn't consider risk or position of the supplier in the wider market

91. Stakeholder Allegiance Matrix

The Stakeholder Allegiance Matrix considers stakeholders in a project based upon their understanding of the project and their level of agreement. Determining where in the model a stakeholder sits, helps identify the strategy required to embrace, ignore or overcome them.

The Stakeholder Allegiance Matrix is a well-established positioning model to help managers understand the stance taken by different stakeholders in a project enabling strategy to be developed to manage the different factions and help ensure optimum project delivery.

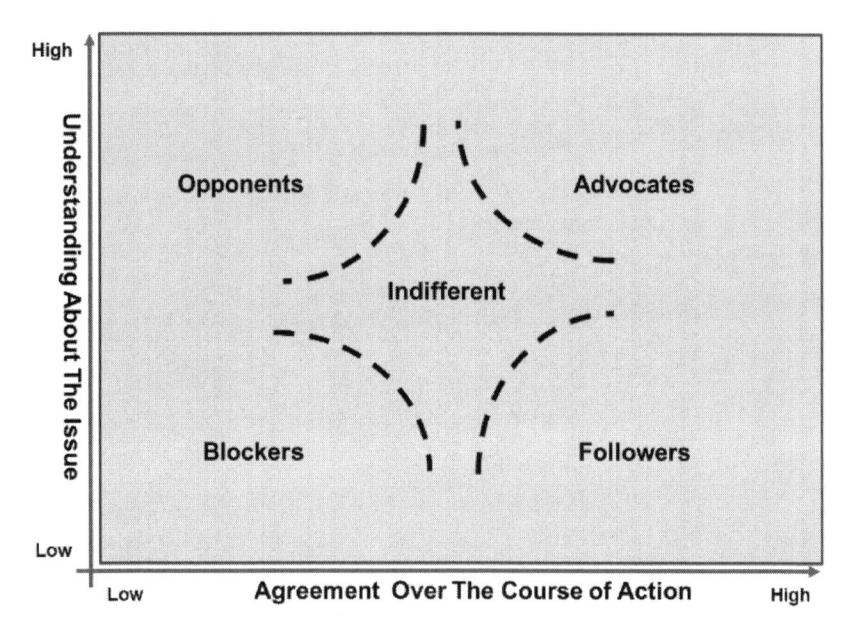

[Diagram: A matrix with Y-axis "Understanding About The Issue" (Low to High) and X-axis "Agreement Over The Course of Action" (Low to High). Four quadrants labelled: Opponents (top-left), Advocates (top-right), Blockers (bottom-left), Followers (bottom-right), with Indifferent in the centre.]

A good project manager will understand that enforcement with stakeholders is only one approach; coaching, capitulation and enticement are other possible approaches that can be used to help steer the project to a successful completion.

Positive Views on Model	Negative Views on Model
Easy to understand positioning model • Enables clear determination of strategy in many cases	• Can pigeonhole stakeholders, and address positions with generic approaches • Labelling a group not conducive to a successful outcome

92. Supplier Relationship Management (SRM) Interface

The Supplier Relationship Management(SRM) Interface model looks at how SRM and related Supply Chain functions are interrelated rather than linear and separate, as was traditionally the case. The procurement function generally owns the SRM governance model and processes, and facilitates the development of a cross-functional SRM capability.

Twice as many SRM leaders as followers (61%) have cross-functional teams assigned to strategic suppliers – an essential component in ensuring that relationships are managed in a consistent and co-ordinated way. Further, Leaders typically have full-time dedicated SRM managers in place for these relationships.

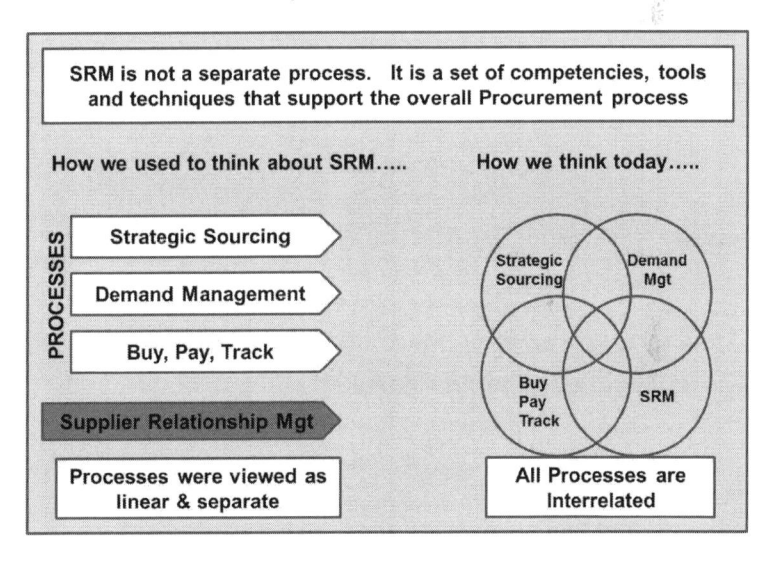

```
SRM is not a separate process. It is a set of competencies, tools
and techniques that support the overall Procurement process
```

How we used to think about SRM.....   How we think today.....

PROCESSES:
- Strategic Sourcing
- Demand Management
- Buy, Pay, Track
- Supplier Relationship Mgt

Processes were viewed as linear & separate

Today (Venn diagram): Strategic Sourcing, Demand Mgt, Buy Pay Track, SRM — All Processes are Interrelated

Leading organisations such as Proctor & Gamble invest heavily in training for these staff, with a focus on interpersonal skills such as communications, trust building, change management and cross-functional working.

Positive Views on Model	Negative Views on Model
• Recognised as being essential in terms of the successful implementation of SRM • Widely used in organisations	• Some users believe it is lacking in detail

93. Thomas & Kilmann Conflict Mode Instrument

The Thomas & Kilmann Conflict Mode Instrument uses a binary questionnaire to determine the specific characteristics of an individual and their approach to conflict styles and resolution approaches.

The Thomas & Kilmann Model was first presented in 1974 and uses a detailed thirty question binary two-option questionnaire. The model has some links to the 1960's model by Blake & Mouton and identifies five strategic approaches to evaluate and manage the conflict in a situation.

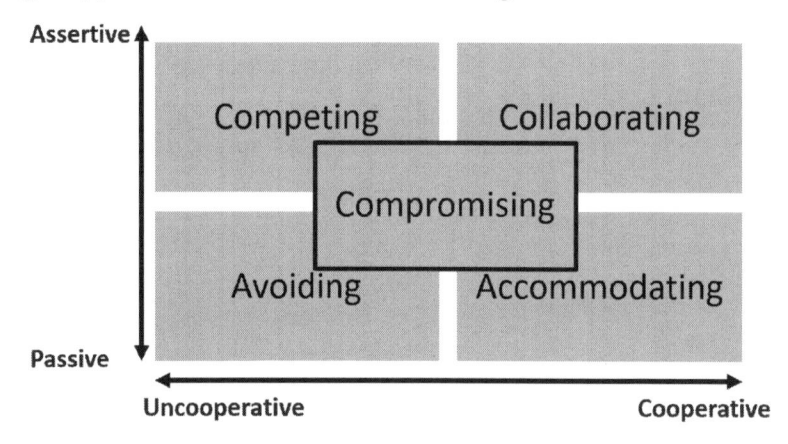

```
Assertive ▲
         │   Competing        Collaborating
         │         ┌──────────────────┐
         │         │  Compromising    │
         │         └──────────────────┘
         │    Avoiding         Accommodating
Passive  ▼
         ◄─────────────────────────────────►
         Uncooperative              Cooperative
```

Further, the model has also been linked with the Kraljic Matrix (see Model 71) highlighting potential approaches to dialogue and conflict in the respective quadrants, as well as with communication styles:
- Competing aligned with Aggressive dialogue with Leverage suppliers
- Collaborating aligned with Assertive dialogue with Strategic suppliers
- Avoiding aligned with Avoidance of dialogue with Routine suppliers
- Accommodating aligned with an Accommodating dialogue with Bottleneck Suppliers
- Compromising is the middle ground with alignment with all the Kraljic Quadrants

Positive Views on Model	Negative Views on Model
• Well regarded model with good substantiating questionnaire • Aligns with other models such as Kraljic	• Use of the questionnaire is chargeable • There are a lot of competing Occupational Personality Questionnaires

Risk

94. Business Continuity Planning
95. Four T Model of Risk
96. Risk Cycle
97. Risk-Impact Model

94. Business Continuity Planning

Business Continuity Planning (BCP) is the process of understanding, evaluating and preparing strategy to ensure that a business is not interrupted from delivering its core objectives. In addition to pre-emptive activity, a BCP plan includes Disaster Recovery activity to ensure a speedy resolution is achieved in the event that the worst does occur.

Business Continuity Planning is a function closely associated with the general risk management function, and addresses the specific risks that, could prevent an organisation from undertaking its contractual and critical obligations. The key measure of success is the resilience to risk

The list of risks is generated within the normal risk management process, and evaluated against their impact and probability. These dimensions are then assessed in more depth within the BCP Cycle below:

The Five Step process starts with a detailed analysis of the situation to help generate a prevention and remedial solution. This is implemented, tested and accepted, and then maintained over the life of the BCP process. Maintenance of the process involves updating the critical risk log and review of the remedial strategies and their fitness for purpose.

Positive Views on Model	Negative Views on Model
• Dovetails well with risk process and concepts such as SPOF analysis • Generates solutions for Force *Majeure Risks*	• There are often blurred lines between BCP and normal risk process

95. Four T Model of Risk

The Four T Model of Risk looks at ways in which risk can be dealt with as part of the corporate strategy. The risk can be: Tolerated, Treated, Transferred or Terminated.

The Four T Model of Risk recognises that in an organisation there will be various different types of risk, and that with a limited budget and operational practicalities not all of the risks can be fully dealt with all of the time. With this understood, the Risk Manager must examine the risks, determine the impact and probability, to establish a hierarchy of risks which need to be addressed.

Once prioritised, the risk strategy can be implemented with this model suggesting four core categories of risk strategy that they will fall into and is more structured than a traditional Pareto approach where there may be a simple line drawn with risk above dealt with and risk below ignored:

Treat
- Introduce process or resource to **Treat** and negate the risk

Transfer
- Use contractual relationships or insurance policies to **Transfer** risk to someone else

Tolerate
- Examine the risk and **Tolerate** it, but reviewing the risk on a regular basis

Terminate
- Take action to **Terminate** the risk so it is no longer going to affect the organisation

Positive Views on Model	Negative Views on Model
• Clear strategy given to each identified risk • Easy to remember and apply	• May be other options or strategies to deal with the risk

96. Risk Cycle

The Risk Cycle highlights the various stages of the risk management process from identification through addressing the risk and onward monitoring. Once in process and monitored, a review of the risk remedies and the risks affecting the situation should again be assessed.

The Risk Cycle considers risk from identification through various stages to the mitigation and review. Risk is however ever-changing, so once in place and monitored the risk management solution will already be reviewing the probability of an occurrence, the impact, the success of the mitigation process and any side effects caused by the mitigation process.

For example, to reduce the risk of a major fire, a sprinkler system may be installed, but with this comes the risk of a false activation destroying computer equipment so are files backed-up? Fire extinguishers could be used instead but what if they are used to prop fire-doors open?

- Identify the Risk and its origins
- Understand the Risk
- Long term Impact of the Risk
- Strategies to Combat the Risk
- Select Risk Response and Actions
- Monitor and Report Outcomes

Positive Views on Model	Negative Views on Model
• Structured approach to risk • Drives strategy and process	• No ideas directly just process orientation • Risk different for every organisation and structure

97. Risk-Impact Model

The Risk-Impact Model is used to assess and categorise the severity of the risk associated with a situation based on the likely impact of the risk, and the probability that the risk may occur.

The Risk-Impact Model analyses the relationship between the probability that a risk will occur and the consequences and impact that the occurrence will cause to the organisation in question.

The probability of the risk occurring will be based on a number of different facets including statistical analysis, forecast data, historical experience and input from core stakeholders. This information generates a prediction as to how often an event will occur, enabling the organisation to decide whether remedial action is required. If remediation is undertaken the scenario is reassessed to determine the adjusted probability.

Equally important is the cost or impact an occurrence will have on an organisation, referred to in the model as "severity of impact". This may be a financial loss due to the cost of repairing the damage, the loss of sales or customers, the cost of downtime or loss of reputation.

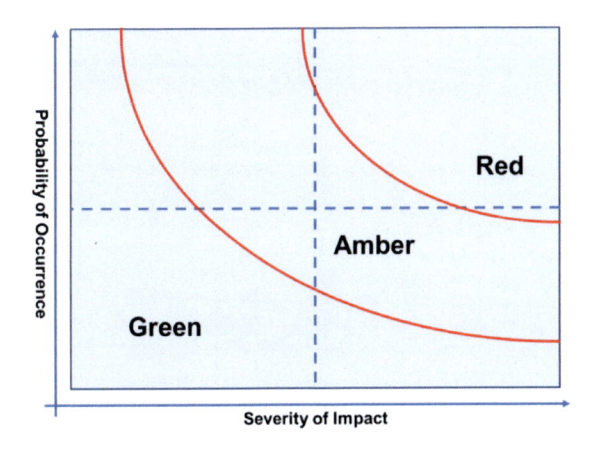

Plotting the data within the grid enables the risk to be categorised as Red (highest), Amber or Green (lowest) in line with the segments shown. Once categorised, if required, risk can be more easily managed against generic policy.

Positive Views on Model	Negative Views on Model
• Good for prioritising risk in an easy to understand format • Helps with an initial assessment of where to focus time and effort	• Doesn't identify risk, only categorises it • No real output other than a categorisation of risk in one of three levels

Strategic Supply Chain Management

98. Bhattacharya Outsourcing Decision Model
99. Christopher & Towill Lean Agile Matrix
100. Cousins Strategic Supply Wheel
101. Goldratt Theory of Constraints
102. Inventory Decision Matrix

98. Bhattacharya Outsourcing Decision Model

The Bhattacharya Outsourcing Decision Model looks at the options available when an organisation is contemplating outsourcing a process or service. It considers two variables, namely the risk exposure of the supplier capability and the risk exposure of the client capability.

A process/service should be outsourced when the risk exposure of a supplier capability to deliver the service is lower than, or equal to that of the buying organisation. The model highlights the relationship between the risk exposure of the two parties.

In quadrant 1, risk exposure of the Supplier capability is low, and that of the Client is high, so it will be prudent to outsource. Outsourcing is also a valid option when both parties have low risk as in quadrant 2, although in this instance, the client should outsource to enable it to focus on aspects which it is good at an generate a more favourable return. When the risk exposure of the client is low and the supplier's high, then in-house is optimal as in quadrant 4. In some situations when both have high risk, it may be prudent to develop capabilities in-house whilst supporting suppliers to develop capabilities as in quadrant 3.

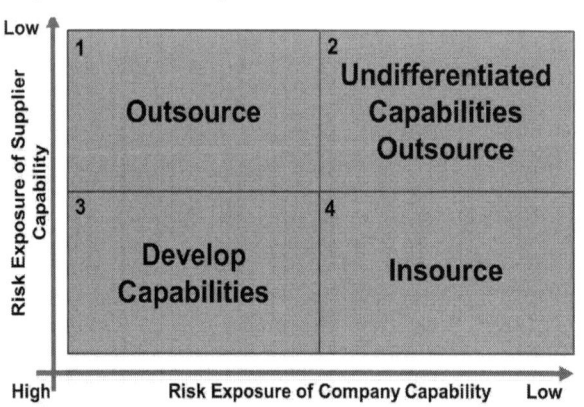

	Low Risk Exposure of Company Capability	High Risk Exposure of Company Capability
Low Risk Exposure of Supplier Capability	1. Outsource	2. Undifferentiated Capabilities Outsource
High Risk Exposure of Supplier Capability	3. Develop Capabilities	4. Insource

The effectiveness of this model is predicated by the ability of the Client to effectively assess the relative risks accurately. However, it does focus the mind in terms of risk assessment of outsourcing.

Positive Views on Model	Negative Views on Model
• Gives clear direction based on the corporate risk profile	• Doesn't consider issues such as market trends or resource availability • Similar models exist see Greaver (1999)

99. Christopher & Towill Lean-Agile Matrix

The Christopher and Towill Lean-Agile Matrix model was developed to identify if a Lean or Agile solution should be adopted by an organisation based on its product characteristics and the demand profile for the products.

The Lean-Agile Matrix is used to understand the mix between adopting a Lean solution with a focus on: 1. maintaining a low or zero inventory; 2. manufacturing product to order, 3. versus having an Agile, flexible catalogue or product set which can be made quickly to a customer's specific requirements.

Level of Product Standardisation ↑	**Inventory Based Supply Chain Solution** Useful where the product types tend to be generic items for example procured against a standard part number, but demand profile is uncertain	**Lean Supply** A stable demand profile and product mix leads to a focus on making product quickly to order as opposed to delivery from stock. Focus is on low or zero inventory with JIT supply of materials.
	Agile Solution Used with unpredictable demand, with products adopting bespoke features or are specific client needs. Common components or part finished assemblies used with late customisation used.	**Hybrid Solution** Where there is a clear and predictable demand pattern, but solutions are bespoke, specially designed for the application, or customised to the clients specific requirements

Predictability and Stability of Demand →

In addition, in some cases a compromise solution may be sought as in adopting a solution which relies on inventory (used where demand is erratic and/or there are long or unpredictable Supply Chains) or adopting close partnership solutions with consultants, architects or designers (often retained as an internal resource) which allow predictable demand for bespoke solutions to be produced in an efficient and timely fashion.

Positive Views on Model	Negative Views on Model
• Easy to understand four box model used to steer thinking • Identifies the core differences between concepts	• Suggests there is a clear two-dimensional argument yet other factors have a clear influence

100. Cousins Strategic Supply Wheel

The Cousins Strategic Supply Wheel outlines six key factors that a Procurement and Supply professional faces and must consider individually and collectively when forming a corporate and supply relationship strategy.

The Strategic Supply Wheel stresses the importance of aligning corporate and procurement policies. A lack of connectivity makes it extremely difficult, if not impossible, for Procurement professionals to set their own polices, objectives and strategies whilst reflecting the needs, wants and direction of the organisation itself. The overall focus of the organisation, whether it is cost, quality or differentiation, will dictate the corporate and, therefore, procurement strategy.

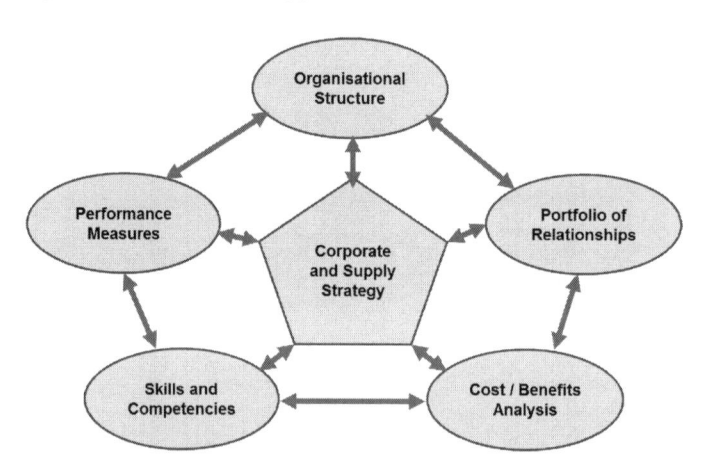

```
                    Organisational
                      Structure
                         |
        Performance      |      Portfolio of
         Measures ---- Corporate ---- Relationships
                    and Supply
                     Strategy
                         |
         Skills and      |      Cost / Benefits
        Competencies ----+---- Analysis
```

Procurement departments are typically given a high focus on cost reduction in organisations but should also have a major role in maintaining quality aspirations and on time delivery. Tactical methods of cost reduction with short to medium-term relationships are often favoured over more complex long-term relationships yet development of aspects such as measurement strategy, organisational structure and training all of which are key to success.

Positive Views on Model	Negative Views on Model
• Identifies core elements for attention and development within corporate strategy	• No reference to culture or the organisation's willingness to accept change

101. Goldratt Theory of Constraints

The Goldratt Theory of Constraints concept suggests achievable goals may be set, yet constraints will always restrict achievement. Overcoming these constraints through continuous investigation and improvement is the secret to success.

The Goldratt Theory of Constraints was proposed by Goldratt in the late 1970s and suggested that an organisation would always be held back by its inability to overcome every constraint in its operating environment. Overcoming or addressing constraints would help the organisation achieve more of its goals, albeit that it may have to dramatically rethink or restructure its business operations to achieve this. Failure to address these constraints would mean that the organisation can never fulfil its true theoretical full potential, and whilst it has an issue – an "Achilles Heel" – it would always be vulnerable from hostile activity, uncertainty and risk.

To understand a constraint, the growth of value and throughput was examined. Paradoxically, growth cannot carry on to infinity therefore there must be a constraining factor at all times. As the goal of the organisation is usually to increase shareholder wealth, measurement of turnover and costs are key to this being achieved, both are finite concepts. To overcome these constraints, the organisation needs to adopt a philosophy of continuous review, investigation and improvement, this Goldratt called the "Thinking Process" and follows five steps:

1. Identify what and where the constraint is;
2. Assess the constraint and decide on how to address it;
3. Focus on achieving these first two actions at the expense of others;
4. Evaluate the constraint and monitor it in an operational context;
5. Repeat if the constraint is overcome with the new constraint that replaces the first.

Positive Views on Model	Negative Views on Model
- Useful model in manufacturing and project scenarios - Needs clarity of goals to help focus on the constraints	- Perceived by some as being unduly pessimistic - Competition used by some Not-For-Profit groups instead of constraining theories

102. Inventory Decision Matrix

The Inventory Decision Matrix is a four box model which assesses the inventory decision process based on two core factors affecting inventory; the impact of a stock-out and the ease and speed with which the product can be sourced in the market. The model goes on to highlight ways to reduce inventory through addressing the impact and sourcing issues.

The Inventory Decision Model considers inventory decisions based on two dimensions – the impact on the organisation of a stock-out versus the ease with which the item can be obtained in the market – and promotes strategy to reduce impact and improve the ease of sourcing. These two dimensions combine to steer the stock or otherwise decision making process.

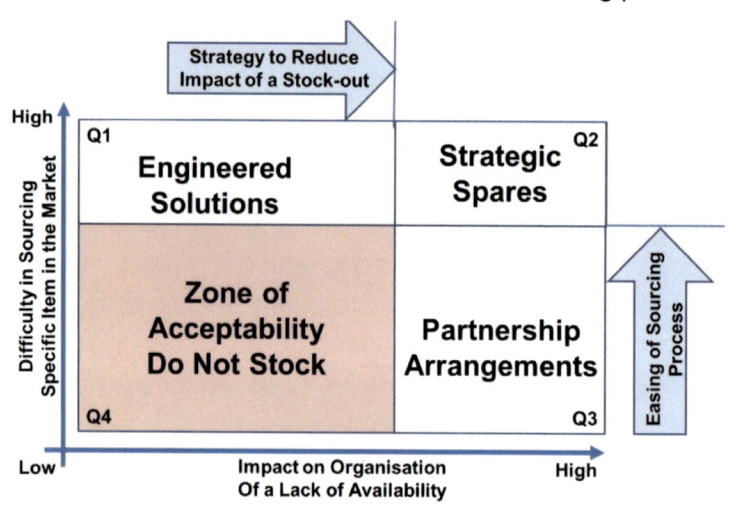

Diagram: Inventory Decision Matrix

- Y-axis: Difficulty in Sourcing Specific Item in the Market (Low to High)
- X-axis: Impact on Organisation Of a Lack of Availability (Low to High)
- Q1 (High difficulty, Low impact): Engineered Solutions
- Q2 (High difficulty, High impact): Strategic Spares
- Q4 (Low difficulty, Low impact): Zone of Acceptability – Do Not Stock
- Q3 (Low difficulty, High impact): Partnership Arrangements
- Arrows: "Strategy to Reduce Impact of a Stock-out" and "Easing of Sourcing Process"

Accordingly, once the core observations of the Inventory Decision Matrix have been implemented as directed by the four box directives, the longer term effort for an organisation looking to control its own destiny, should be to draw as much dependent and independent demand as possible into the bottom left quadrant as shaded through strategy to reduce the impact of a stock out and focused on overcoming the sourcing obstacles.

Positive Views on Model	Negative Views on Model
• Addresses the core drivers of inventory	• Doesn't directly differentiate between dependent and independent inventory

Conclusion

Following the success and positive feedback from our first edition coupled with the review of a number of the major academic syllabi, we have endeavoured to provide an updated perspective of some of the most popular models in modern Procurement and Supply Chain Management whilst at the same time reflecting the needs of the practitioner. This has been done in the same way as with the first edition – 101 Models of Procurement and Supply Chain Management – with a clear focus on having just one page per model to ensure a succinctness commensurate with the student and practitioner mandates.

As will have been evident from the contents, many of the models are intended to generate thought or collate ideas, some produce meaningful output in their own right, whilst others are merely used to communicate or illustrate an idea, concept or strategy. This book is intended to decipher the mystique, bestow the virtues and highlight the pitfalls of academic theories and models so that the reader can decide which, if any, they will use in their exams or within their day-to-day work activities.

Whether transmitting a message within or outside the organisation, communication skills will be of paramount importance, in many instances shaping, making or breaking the message. Models need to be incorporated into an effective communication strategy, embedded in a wider proposal or used to underpin a point in an exam or thesis. Use of effective communication methods is often as important as the message itself, with the use of dynamic and innovative graphs, images, and other graphics to illustrate a point, see below.

Reference: *101 Charts That Sell: Bars, Pies, Lines, and More Graphs to Persuade in your Workplace.*

When transmitting this message, think outside the box; use inventive graphics as above, or English literacy techniques such as Onomatopoeia, Alliteration, Assonance and Metaphors, or techniques from the great orators of history.

Further, think about simplistic messages. As detailed in the POINT model, a human mind cannot take in and remember complicated images or text; there is the Power of Three concept that suggests you should never use more than three colours, three types, sizes, or styles of text as this will overload the brain and the message will be diminished. Politicians use this when speaking, often giving three reasons for something and often use techniques such as PREP (Point-Reason-Example-Point) when speaking to make a Point, explain it, give credibility with an example, before reiterating the Point; in exams perhaps this concept could be adapted to the word PREM - Point-Reason-Example-Model - to maximise the marks secured!

Life and business are far from simplistic but these models, to some extent, go some way to helping unravel and explain the concepts and theories of organisations, Procurement and the Supply Chain.

And remember, in exams, "Models Mean Marks".

Model Resources

Business Model	Primary References
Business Analysis	
Ansoff Planning Model	Strategic Management, Ansoff 1979
Balanced Scorecards	Balanced Scorecard: Translating Strategy into Action, Kaplan & Norton 1996
Critical Needs Analysis (CNA)	Needs Assessment, Kaufman et al 1993
Pareto Analysis	Cours d'Économie Politique Professé a l'Université de Lausanne, Pareto 1896
PEST / PESTLE / STEEPLE / STEEPLED Analysis	ETPS Analysis, Aguilar 1967
SWOT Analysis & TOWS Strategy Model	Stanford Reseacrh Institute, Humphrey 1961
Category Management	
AT Kearney Seven Step Category Management Model	AT Kearney 2001
Bartolini Scorecard	Ardent Partners Bartolini 2015
CIPS Category Management Model	CIPS Construct 2012
Jackson & Crocker Category Management Model	CIPS Paper, Jackson & Crocker 2017
OSCAR Model	CIPS Category Management Study Guide 2015
Contract & Change Management	
ADR	Principles of Alternative Dispute Resolution, Ware 2016
Carter 6S Contract Management Model	Practical Procurement, Carter, Jackson et al
Kotter 8 Phases of Change	Leading Change, Kotter 1996

Business Model	Primary References
Lewin Freeze & Force Field Analysis Models	Frontiers in Group Dynamics, Lewin 1947
Parker Supplier Performance Review (SUPER) Model	Unpublished Paper, Parker 2019
Cost & Value	
Activity Based Costing	Time Driven Activity Based Costing, Kaplan & Anderson 2003
Kano Model	Attractive Quality and Must-be Quality, Kano 1982
Porter Value Chain	Competitive Advantage: Creating and Sustaining Superior Performance, Porter 1985
Total Cost of Ownership Model	Procurement Principles and Management, Bailey Farmer Crocker 2016
Value Analysis & Value Stream Mapping	Techniques of Value Analysis and Engineering, Miles 1961
Ethical & Environmental	
8R Model of Responsible Waste Treatment	The Gaia Foundation 8R Concept
4D Model	CFA Institute Conflict of Interest Guidance Notes
Green Diversity Model	CIPD Diversity & Inclusion at Work, 2018
Inequality -Types and Principles	Equality Act 2010
Nine Dimensions of Sustainability	The Sustainable Business, Jackson et al 2011
Ohno Seven Wastes	Toyota Production System, Ohno 1988
3E Model	New Public Management (NPM), Aucoin & Pollit 1990
3i Model	Moral Prohibitions & Concent, Brock 1980

Model Resources

Business Model	Primary References
Human Resource Management	
Belbin Team Roles	Team Roles at Work, Belbin 1997
Crocker Triangle	Excellence in Supplier Management, Emmett & Crocker 2009
Eysenck Hierarchical Model of Personality	Dimensions of Personality, Eysenck 1947
Goleman's Domains of Emotional Intelligence	Emotional Intelligence, Goleman 1995
Hofstede Cultural Factors Model	Cultural Consequences, Hofstede 1983
Honey & Mumford Learning Styles	Manual of Learning Styles, Honey & Mumford 1982
HR RITUAL	The Sustainable Business, Jackson et al 2011
Johnson Cultural Web	Exploring Corporate Strategy, Johnson & Scholes 1992
RACI Assessment	Goal Directed Project Management Grug, Haug &Andersen 1984
Rodgers Seven Point Plan	Seven point Plan NIIP, Rodgers 1974
Training Needs Analysis - Vanguard Model	Vanguard Method, Seddon 1987
Management & Leadership	
Adair Action-Centred Leadership Model	Action-Centred Leadership, Adair 1973
Ashridge Management Styles	Leadership Styles, Sadler & Hofstede 1976
Cialdini Six Principles of Persuasion	Influence, Cialdini 2001
Fayol Principles of Management	General and Industrial Management, Fayol 1930
Greiner Growth Model	Evolution and revolution as Organisations Grow, Greiner 1998

Business Model	Primary References
Hersey-Blanchard Model	Management of Organisational Behaviour, Hersey Blanchard 1982
Herzberg Hygiene/Motivators	One More Time - How do you motivate employees, Herzberg 1987
Hierarchy of Objectives	Managing the Implementation of Development Projects, Youker 1998
Maslow Hierarchy of Needs	A Theory of Human Motivation, Maslow 1943
McKinsey 7S Model	McKinsey 7S Framework, Peters & Waterman 1980
Mintzberg 5P Model	5Ps for Strategy, Mintzberg 1995
Mintzberg Management Roles	Planning on the Left Side, Managing on the Right, Mintzberg 1976
Mullins Process of Management Model	Management and Organisational Behaviour, Mullins 1999
Nadler and Tushman Congruence Model	Organisational Dynamics, Nadler & Tushman 1980
Organisational Balance Model	Organisational Balance, Foster 2018
Senge Five Disciplines	The Fifth Discipline, Senge 1990
Theory X, Theory Y and Theory Z	The Human Side of Enterprise, McGregor 1960
Trait Theory	Handbook of Leadership: A survey of theory and practice, Stogdill 1974
Trist & Bamforth Socio-Technical Approach	Social and Psychological Consequences of the Long Wall Method of Coal-Getting, Trist & Bamforth 1951
Tuckman Team Development	Developmental Sequence in Small Groups, Tuckman 1965

Model Resources

Business Model	Primary References
Market & Price Analysis	
Ansoff Matrix	Strategies for Diversification, Harvard Business Review, Ansoff 1957
Boston Consulting Group Matrix & Product Lifecycle	Boston Consulting Group (BCG) Matrix, Henderson 1970
Kotler 4P Model	Marketing Management, Kotler & Renshaw 1994
Porter Competitive Advantage Model	Competitive Advantage of Nations. Porter 1985
Porter Five Force Model	Competitive Advantage of Nations. Porter 1985
Supply Market Analysis	Marketing Management: Analysis, Planning and Control, Kotler 1967
Procurement	
Carter 10C Model	Practical Procurement, Carter, Jackson et al 2010
Crocker Simplified Service Gap Model	Excellence in Services Procurement, Crocker et al 2010
Five Rights of Purchasing	Procurement Principles and Management, Bailey Farmer Crocker et al 2016
Iron Triangle Model	Iron Triangle, Barnes 1988
Kraljic Matrix	Purchasing Must Become Supply Management, Kraljic 1983
Maturity Assessment Model	Crocker unpublished
Monczka MSU Model	Competitive Supply Strategies, Monczka 2000
Steele & Court Supplier Preferencing Model	Profitable Purchasing Strategies, Steele and Court 1996
Syson Positioning Graph - Strategic Policies	Improving Purchasing Performance, Syson 1992
Syson Positioning Graph - Strategic Performance	Improving Purchasing Performance, Syson 1992

Business Model	Primary References
Quality	
Cost of Poor Quality (COPQ) Model	Poor Quality Costs, Harrington 1987
Deming / Shewhart Plan-Do-Check-Act (PDCA)	Out of the Crisis, Deming 1986
EFQM Excellence Model	EFQM Excellence Model, numerous unamed contributors 2013
Fishbone / Root Cause Analysis / Ishikawa Diagram	Guide to Quality Control, Ishikawa 1968
Kaizen	Kaizen: The Key to Japan's Competitive Success, Masaaki 1986
Six Sigma, DMAIC & SIPOC Models	Six Sigma for Managers, Bruce 2005
Voice of the Customer & Quality Circles	Voice of the Customer Capture & Analysis, Kai Yang 2008
Relationships & Stakeholder Management	
Burnes & New Customer/Supplier Relationships	Collaboration in Customer-Supplier Relationships, Burnes &New 1997
Cox Supplier Relationships Management Model	Supplier Relationship Management, Cox et al 2003
Crocker Managing Satisfaction of Service Quality Model	Excellence in Services Procurement, Crocker et al 2010
Customer-Supplier Partnership Bridge	Excellence in Supplier Management, Emmett & Crocker 2009
Egan Stakeholder Positioning (Labels) Model	Working the Shadow Side, Egan 1994
Johnson Supplier Management Behaviours Model	Exploring Corporate Strategy, Johnson & Scholes 2007
Mendelow Matrix	Environmental Scanning: Impact of the Stakeholder Concept, Mendelow 1991

Model Resources

Business Model	Primary References
Relationship Determination Model	Excellence in Supplier Management, Emmett & Crocker 2009
Stakeholder Allegiance Matrix	Proctor & Gamble, 1997
Supplier Relationship Management (SRM) Interfaces	Crocker unpublished, 2010
Thomas & Kilmann Conflict Mode Instrument	The Thomas-Kilmann Conflict Mode Instrument, Thomas & Kilman 1974
Risk	
Business Continuity Planning	Constructing a Successful Business Continuity Plan, Berman 2015
Four T Model of Risk	Defining Risk, Holton 2004
Risk Cycle	Fundamentals of Risk Management: Understanding, Evaluating and Implementing Effective Risk Management, Hopkins 2018
Risk-Impact Model	Identifying and Managing Project Risk : Essential Tools for Failure-Proofing Your Project, Kendrick 2018
Strategic Supply Chain Management	
Bhattacharya Outsourcing Decision Model	Outsourcing Iterative Improvement Model, Bhattacharya 2008
Christopher & Towill Lean Agile Matrix	An Integrated Model for the Design of Agile Chains, Christopher & Towill 2001
Cousins Strategic Supply Wheel	Strategic Supply Management Principles, Cousins et al 2007
Goldratt Theory of Constraints	The Goal, Goldratt 1984
Inventory Decision Matrix	IMPA Magazine, 2018

Secondary References & Wider References

Balanced Scorecard, Olve & Sjostrand, 2006

Blue Ocean Strategy, Chan Kim & Mauborgne

Careers Guidance in Context, Gothard 2001

Category Management in Purchaing, O'Brien 2009

CIPS Code of Conduct

CIPS & Profex Study Guides 2004-2019

Competitive Advantage of Nations, 1985

Cours d'Économie Politique Professé a l'Université de Lausanne, Pareto Vol. II 1897

CPO Rising, July 2012

Cut Carbon Grow Profit, Tang & Yeoh 2007

Essentials of Balanced Scorecards, Kaplan & Norton 1992

Essentials of Balanced Scorecards, Nar 2004

Excellence in Global Supply Chain Management, Emmett & Crocker 2010

Exploring Corporate Strategy, Johnson & Scholes 2007

Game Theory and Economic Modelling, Kreps 1990

General and Industrial Management, Storrs 1949

Getting to the Yes, Fisher, Ury & Patton 1991

Green Supply Chains, Emmett & Sood 2010

Herzberg et al The motivation to work (2nd ed.) 1959

IMPA Magazine 2011

Implanting Strategic Management, Ansoff & McDonnell, 1990

Influence, Science & Practice, 2009

Integrated Material Management, Carter & Price 1998

International Studies of Management & Organization, 1976

Into the Upwave, Robert Beckman 1988

kano.plus

Know your own personality, Eysenck & Wilson, 1976

Model Resources

Lean Six Sigma Handbook, Pysdek & Keller 2008

Lean Thinking, Womack & Jones 1996

Learning Organisations in Practice, Pearn & Mulrooney 1995

Management der Marketing-Kommunikation, Fuchs, 2005

Management Teams, Belbin, 1981

Managing Differences in Multicultural Organisations, Hofstede 1980

Marketing Management, Kotler 1994

National Institute of Industrial Psychology 1952

Off the Track: why and how successful executives get derailed, McCall & Lombardo 1983

Operations Rules: Delivering Customer Value, Simchi-Levi 2010

Operations and Supply Chain Management, Chase 2010

Organisational Behaviour, Buchanon & Huczynski 2004

Outsourcing The Human Resource Function, Cook 1998

PMI Government Extension to the PMBOK Guide 3rd Edition 2006

PMI Project Manager Competency Develop't Framework 2nd Ed 2007

Procurement Principles and Management, Bailey Farmer Crocker et al 2016

Purchasing Scams, Trevor Kitching 2001

Sarbanes-Oxley Act 2002

Screw It, Lets Do It, Richard Branson 2007

Simulated Social Skill Training for Interpersonal Professions, Singleton et al 1980

Six Sigma Course Manual, Capella Associates 2011

Six Sigma for Managers, Bruce 2005

Smith & Keenan's Law for Business, 12th Edition 1999

Stores Distribution & Management, Carter, Price & Emmett 2004

Strategy, Harvard Business Essentials 2005

Suppy Chain Excellence, Bolstroff 2007

The Category Management Handbook, Thompson & Cordell 2018

The Constant Economy, Zac Goldsmith 1988

The Emergence of Global Value Chains, OECD Report November 2012

The Emotionally Intelligent Leader, HBR 2019

The Forces of Economic Growth, Greiner 2005

The Journal of Organisational Behaviour, Zahhly & Tosi 1989

The Kondratiev Cycle, Alexander 2001

The Machine that Changed the World, Womack, Jones & Rose 1990

The Performance Prism, Neely, Adams & Kennerley 2002

The Purchasing Chessboard 2008, Schuh, Kromoser et al

The Quest: Energy, Security and the Modern World, Yergin 2006

The Relationship Driven Supply Chain, Emmett & Crocker 2009

The Revoloutionin Purchase, Syson 1989

The Scientific Study of Personality Eysenck, 1952

The Six Sigma Handbook, Pyzdek & Keller 2008

The Story of Lean Production, Womack, Jones & Roos 1990

The Sustainable Business, Jackson et al 2011

The Universal Declaration of Human Rights 1948

The Wiremold Company: A century of solutions, Smith 2001

Theory Z, Ouchi 1981

Tools for the Learning Organisation, Pearn & Mulrooney 2003

Toward an Applied Theory of Experiential Learning, Kolb 1974

TOWS AnalysiosWiehrich 1982

Treat People Right, Lawler & Lawler 2011

Weybrecht 2000

Working with Emotional Intelligenc, Goleman 1998

Journals and Trade Magazines

Association of Consulting Engineers

Institute of Director's publications

Institute of Mechanical Engineer's publications

National Geographic

Supplier Management Magazine

The Economist

The Financial Times and Supplements

Time Magazine

Model Resources

Specific Websites

www.Businessballs.com May 2019

www.study.com/lesson/lewin

www.cips.org/knowledge/procurement-topics-and-skills

www.12manage.com/methods_kano_customer_satisfaction_model

www.lucidchart.com/value-stream-mapping

www.equalityhumanrights.com

www.johnadair.co.uk

www.glynholton.com

www.ecollaboration.org.au 2019/20 Annual Report

www.who.int

www.hbr.org Elkington 2018

www.theleanway.net

www.tandfonline.com

www.belbin.com

www.hult.edu

www,vanguard-method.net

www.businessballs.com